1978

SELECTED ODES

PINDAR

SELECTED ODES

Translated, with Interpretive Essays, by
Carl A. P. Ruck and William H. Matheson

Ann Arbor
THE UNIVERSITY OF MICHIGAN PRESS

To Meta, Bet, and Gordon

Acknowledgments

We wish to express, first, our gratitude to those friends who read parts of the manuscript in various stages of its preparation, and in particular to William Arrowsmith, Sterling Dow, John Finley, Kimon Friar, and James Notopoulos, who encouraged the beginnings of our undertaking. We are especially indebted also to three scholars whom we know only through their writings: Elroy L. Bundy *(Studia Pindarica)*, R.W.B. Burton *(Pindar's Pythian Odes)*, and B.A. Van Groningen *(La Composition littéraire archaïque grecque)*. We must, further, express our especial indebtedness to Gerald Else, who read the entire manuscript and suggested numerous improvements. We deeply appreciate Mrs. Helena Dougherty's assistance in bringing our work to completion. The above people, it need not be said, are not responsible for whatever errors the book may contain. Who, then, is responsible? The translators would blame Pindar but think better of it, particularly since each of them is convinced that any blemishes in the text were caused solely by his collaborator, without whose three years of insults, however, the present work could not have appeared.

Carl A. P. Ruck
William H. Matheson

CONTENTS

Car moi, au fond, je suis un solitaire, je crois que la poésie est faite pour le faste et les pompes suprêmes d'une société constituée où aurait sa place la gloire dont les gens semblent avoir perdu la notion.

—Mallarmé

INTRODUCTION: "Belle Marquise, vos beaux yeux me font . . ."

Why do they lie so? And why are the words always different —or worse, why is it they are nearly always the same?

We have observed —to continue the jeremiad— a multitude (obviously Greek–less, for multitudes no longer know Greek) sit in lumpish silence as they heard read to them Housman's tragedy in parody of Aeschylean style. They do not laugh to hear someone addressed as a "suitably attired in leather boots head of a traveler," because apparently for them it is no parody. For them it is the sort of thing one might expect from Greek literature, along with what they have all already read—the deep-cinctured maidens, ox-eyed Hera, and those well-horsed environs. Our lament is not a mere coup de theatre; we have, in fact, only the purveyors of Greek in translation to blame for the general, complacent acceptance of nonsense. Or is the villain still more insidious, for translators are not born but are trained?

It is the call to arms to claim that a translation must be "literal." Few —not that we shall— will forego the beatific security that comes from a profession of literalness. The errors of literal translators are then not theirs but the original author's; and, moreover, the Englished version recalls to their and their critics' minds what they thought Greek sounded like when they "read" it with their teachers in class.

Actually, they did not "read" it at all, but —for such is the training of classicists— they translated a passage each day to prove not that they comprehended the work but that they had memorized the new vocabulary and had grasped the grammar. A good classroom translation had to display the lexicon's definitions and had to mirror in uninflected English the complexities of the Greek grammatical system. Subjects had to be subjects and ethical datives were scrutinized for their morality. Indeed, the verbal system of Greek with its emphasis on three verbal aspects was converted, to facilitate translation, into the English tense-oriented system. Perfects, for example, could no longer communicate a state but were forced to imply antecedent time-relations. It is of course only by charity that we speak of all this as something that happened in the past. The translator, therefore, has the words and has the grammar; and if he is to awaken that happy feeling of recognition in his critics, he can only attempt, like Monsieur Jourdain, to produce poetry by rearranging the order of the words; and he often falls short of that bourgeois gentilhomme's untaught brilliance.

Before going on, we should pause to see just how literal these literal translators have been. Let us take a passage of some difficulty, in a translation that alone could perhaps be called literal. Any line of Pindar will suffice. We select a section from the Olympian poem written for Hagesias of Syracuse.

REPUTATION
(—or opinion —or idea; it is the object of the sentence)

. . . .
(there is no connective particle, which means that the statement is an excited exclamation or that it is a close explanation of the preceding or that there is an error in the textual tradition, in

2

which case the present sentence
may all belong to the preceding
sentence)

I HAVE   (the verb and subject combined,
as common in Greek; the verb is
present but could have a more
general application)

SOME [reputation] OR OTHER

(the indefinite adjective refers
back to the first word and tempers the assurance with which
the poet began)

ON   (obviously a preposition)

TONGUE   (the object of the preposition;
the case indicates that the reputation is securely sitting on the
tongue and not merely touching
it in some surface fashion)

[of] SHRILL   (the form is dialectal; the adjective refers to a high pitch but
apparently the Greeks found the
sound pleasant; it refers as well
to laments, birds, and grasshop-
pers; the word in this position
amends the meter, which is
faulty in all the manuscripts)

WHETSTONE   (the word is dialectal; it goes
with the adjective shrill; the
case of the two words indicates
that a noun phrase is being used
adjectivally; it could therefore
refer to tongue, that is to say,
a "shrill whetstone tongue," or

to reputation, in which case it would be a "shrill whetstone reputation" which could mean that "I have a reputation for being a whetstone," or that "I have the impression that there is a whetstone on my tongue," or that "I have an idea which is a whetstone")

WHICH/AND

("which" is the reading of the manuscripts; it is dialectal; it could refer to whetstone, tongue, or reputation; "and" represents the mistaken attempt of many scholars to correct the meaning of the passage; the translator must choose, since he obviously cannot translate "which/and"; the relative "which" is the subject of its clause)

ME

(naturally, the same person who spoke as "I" in the verbal form above; he now functions as the object of a verb we do not yet have)

WILLING

(a present participle, agreeing with the preceding me; evidently, the "I" enjoys whatever is happening)

CREEPS UPON/TOWARD
DRAGS FORWARD

(the first is the reading of the manuscripts, the second a widely adopted emendation

4

based on the reading of an ancient scholar; it is the verb of which "me" is the object and for which the subject is ambiguous, being either the confused antecedent of the relative or some word in the previous clause)

[with] BEAUTIFUL-FLOWING

(the form is dialectal, or, rather, poetic; it is usually an epithet of water but it is here apparently used metaphorically)

BREATHINGS

(it is the noun for the preceding adjective; its case indicates either accompaniment, that is to say, "with beautiful-flowing breathings," or instrument, that is to say, "by means of beautiful-flowing breathings." What are these beautiful-flowing breathings? The breathing could be poetic inspiration, although the word does not have that meaning yet in Pindar, or the breathing may refer to the process by which the flute is voiced, in which case we have here a metaphor for music, although music is perhaps incompatible with that earlier whetstone which is sharpening my tongue)

GRANDMOTHER

(if we had accepted the reading "and" above, "grandmother" now becomes the subject, and it is she who is either creeping upon us or dragging us forward; if we read "which" above, we already have a subject for that verb and "grandmother," since she is a subject-form, must be the beginning of a new sentence, and we as translators must add the full stop after "breathings" which is lacking in the text. There is, however, difficulty if "grandmother" begins a new sentence, for there is no connective particle —but then, there wasn't any for "reputation" either; we should add that grandmother is on the maternal side, although we do not make such distinctions in English easily, and that she is, moreover, dialectal)

MY

(the adjective identifies the grandmother as belonging to that person who spoke as "I" above; the word is dialectal)

STYMPHALIAN

(the adjective further identifies the grandmother as coming from this place in Arcadia; in Greek, however, two nouns, or a noun and an adjective in certain positions, can comprise a complete sentence; if we start therefore a new sentence with grandmother, we must interpret these words as saying: "My grandmother is Stymphalian";

6

otherwise, it is a Stymphalian grandmother who is creeping upon me, breathing down my neck, and giving me all that pleasure)

WELL-FLOWERED

(the adjective agrees with grandmother, who now suffers metamorphosis into a garden, it appears)

METOPE

(that's her name! it is, of course, dialectal)

HORSE-BEATER

(the form is dialectal; the case is objective and there is as yet nothing for it to agree with)

WHICH

(the relative, in a dialectal form; its antecedent must be grandmother)

THEBE

(the nymph whose name in the plural designates the city of Thebes; the form is dialectal and the objective case relieves the question engendered by "horse-beater": it is she who beats horses)

BORE

(the verb is punctual, that is, not progressive, in the past tense and it supplies the action for the relative; evidently, Metope gave birth to Thebe, who therefore must be Pindar's mother; we are, of course, in the presence of a metaphor, since Pindar came from Thebes; we may assume that the "I" is Pindar, unless he is speaking in the persona of his chorus, which also may have traveled from Thebes)

WHOSE
(dialectal relative, referring evidently to Thebe)

BELOVED
(an adjective for a not-yet-announced noun)

WATER
(it is the water that is beloved, although we do not as yet know whether it is the subject or the object, since the form is ambiguous)

I SHALL DRINK
(the verb with its included subject removes the possibility that water is the subject; we now understand that I shall drink the water; the future tense of the verb causes difficulty, since, in such a structure, the epinician poet often uses a future for a present; the water that is drunk, inasmuch as it comes from Thebes, is a common metaphor in Pindar for poetry: he means that he will compose, or he is composing, a poem; we must add that an unfortunate placement of the relative in a recent translation makes it refer to horses, that is to say, that the poet is drinking horse urine; restrictive or nonrestrictive, it is still horse urine).

8

Introduction

That, then, is your literal translation. With a minimum of Jourdainese, we have what would be considered brilliant in the classroom: "I have some reputation or other on my tongue, a shrill whetstone one, which drags me complacent with my will with beautiful-flowing breathings: my maternal grandmother is Stymphalian; she is well-flowered Metope who bore horse-beater Thebe, whose beloved water I shall drink." Two things are obvious. First, we have, of course, in this literal translation, already made certain decisions about the text. It is, for example, not the grandmother who is doing the stealthy creeping. Second, a daily exercise of this sort does not produce an aesthetic apperception in the translator and his critic. Even our designation of the above as a "literal" translation is a falsification, however, for there are things in the original which we have not caught. No attempt has been made to reproduce the meter (and if we had attempted, it would of necessity have been an English stress-rhythm, rather than the pitch-oriented recitative and quantitative meter of Greek), nor have we spoken of the lost musical and chore-ographic accompaniment. Perhaps still worse than that, we have seen the translated statement as a somewhat isolated phenomenon —as it usually is seen, it seems— and have not heard it in the context, first, of the entire ode, and then as a variation on certain mannerisms of the poet and certain clichés of the genre.

We must admit, therefore, that such "literal" translation is neither desirable nor possible. The poem could not have sounded like *that* to Pindar's audience; the passage may be intimate or humorous, but it was not ridiculous, nor was it, as Van Groningen has cautioned us, a *"fatras d'idées."* It said something and it said it beautifully.

There are two ways of coping with the situation. We can, as some recent translators of Greek have done, assume that the original was too ugly for the modern ear; they have seen their task as one of complete re-creation in the modern idiom, so that the poem will sound no different from something written by a contemporary. Such a translator often dispenses with the impossibilities of the text and works from a version such as the above Jourdainese, either one printed in a trot, like the Loeb, or one prepared for him by friends. We shall parody, to avoid paying royalties:

> Here it is —I have it now!— shrill screechings —ow!
> that whetstone grinds
> my tongue, o tongue: she comes, it drags, she pulls, it
> creeps
> and panting breath and flowing streams (delight
> delights!):
> Mother of mother, grandmother, that is, she's mine, my
> mother's,
> Stymphalian (what else can I do with it?) sowing her
> flowers,
> and it's up! with a sprouting symphony,
> METOPE!
> like temple wall —
> those horses beat, not hers, but hers,
> Thebe-city-nymph was born.   I love,
> I drink, o drink, and drink,
> The welling whorling water wreaths.

The other way is more dangerous. It does not attempt the wholesale importation of well-horsed environs —we have seen that the language did not communicate like that to the Greeks in any case —but neither does it turn its back on the original. The translation must not excessively offend the reader, but it must speak, nevertheless, with the unique voice of Pindar or whatever author one is translating. The translated work must, as R. P. Blackmur has said, add to the available stock of reality. Anything less than this high function would be merely to pander to the contemporary monochrome and to convince the adolescent girl that there still is *something* she can learn from Shakespeare. We wish to see Pindar not with our own eyes but with his, or, failing that, at least with his audience's. We want to feel what we have never felt before and to be, imperfectly, of course, a fifth-century Greek; or better yet, we wish to be he as well as we —a super-audience for the poem. The translation must present a stimulus which must motivate a response—not just any aesthetic response, but the one valid for the particular work and time. We want Bach on the harpsichord with correct ornamentation; we do not want it souped-up in the Romantic style. The translator must therefore stand as a witness —we might almost say as a martyr, for it is the same word—: he has shared, as he thinks, the poet's vision and now will testify to what he has seen. Translators may disagree, for the total vision is greater than they —but the translator must have seen something or else he is merely putting words on paper. As with a witness, the one who is truthful, who adds the minimum of his own elaboration, is the one whose testimony we would prefer. Or to change metaphors, the translator is a screen, a window between the reader and the author. He must efface himself; he must become as transparent as possible, for an opaque window, however intricately decorated, blocks the view. We can read, for example, translations by Pound only as more poetry by Pound.

No matter who the translator, he has made a choice, a selection of what he thinks worthy of translation in a particular work. Will he attempt the meter? Or is it the word-order that is most interesting? To be more specific, we have at times caught the total meaning and the sequence of words, but have disregarded the grammatical connections of the Greek in favor of some English grammatical structure; the words convey the succession of images that the poet had chosen, whereas the grammar was just the means of locating the images in a communication. We would consider such a translation literal, although it does not demonstrate our grasp of the grammar (actually it *does*). At other times it is a mark of punctuation which is the true translation of a phrase in Greek. The dialect we have not chosen to translate, since dialects in English are regional and, for the most part, unsophisticated, whereas Pindar's Dorian was a conscious art-language with a well-developed poetic tradition. It may be, however, that we sometimes catch a nuance of dialect by a moderate sprinkling of "poetic," art nouveau words, tossed, as Howard Nemerov has said, into the Victorian computer. . . . And so on.

Such a translation would, however, produce only a seventh-elaboration Jourdainese. We return to the grandmother. Before the passage can be translated, it must be understood. Unfortunately, there is only one commentary available which is more than a blatant helper for schoolboys; and the author of that work is more interested in hero-cults than in the total meaning of a poem. Most recent books on Pindar, moreover, were written in the wake of Wilamowitz' monumental study, which, however, is based on the false belief that the critic can or should re-create from the poems the poet's life, or read a hypothesized life back into the poems. We have found the ancient Greek annotations to the texts in many cases as useful as most modern works. The translator must therefore first play the role of scholar. But before he can study the text, he must have a text to study, or rather, as his interpretation of the poem begins to emerge in his mind, the various textual possibilities precipitate out into one preferable reading. We have therefore used no one published Greek text, although our line-divisions correspond to the colometric indications in Bowra's Oxford edition. The grandmother, then, must take her place in the entire poem. The translator must understand the theme that the poet is elaborating, and then he must translate so that a variation sounds like a variation of *something*. No literalness will save him if the melody is lost in background noise. The musical terminology is purposefully chosen, for, as the reader will see, Pindar's art plays, in the manner of baroque music, virtuoso ornamentations upon traditional commonplaces, or his melodic basis. It is the interaction of these thematic sections and their variations that produces the poem's communication. A discordant note will do worse than disrupt the harmony, for it will serve to annihilate the poem's meaning and structure. In fact, such discord is what has given so many the impression that Pindar is both meaningless and formless.

The melodies were commonplace ideas for Pindar's contemporaries; they are not so for us. Pindar's contemporaries reacted automatically to his baroque manner; we do not. A translation alone, therefore, cannot by any placement or choice of words stimulate the valid aesthetic experience. The reader must submit to a certain indoctrination, a certain preparation. It is for this purpose that we have broadened the normal concept of a translator's role and included preparatory essays which, like Charles Ives's *Essays Before a Sonata,* are not ancillary but are part of the total composition. The essays are poem oriented and although, tangentially, they attempt to introduce the reader to late archaic Greek poetry, no information is given that does not enhance the particular ode. There is no overall organization, moreover, except that we move from simpler to more complex structures; such corresponds closely to our order of composition, for the translating process became an intense learning situation. Nor could we rewrite all the essays with the knowledge we had gained at the end, for one's acquaintance with a great poet continues to live, and if we had continued to translate, no doubt the last would still in part have negated the last that is here presented. There has been no one procedure, but a constant experimentation. Structural considerations, for example, which in the first poems are discussed in the essays (the long "Pythia IV" was placed first not because it was the best poem but because it showed in a more mechanical fashion and at greater length the technique that we came to appreciate in more subtle occurrences), were later played into the translation itself, where we tried, by typographical means, to convey the divisions and perhaps even the movement of the dance that accompanied the ode. In a higher sense the piecemeal presentation prevents our handing over a coherent aperçu of Pindar, for each reader, as he experiences the odes, will evolve that for himself.

Literal translation, therefore, as we have used it, is faithful to more than just the words, and certainly to more than just the grammatical structure. It must sense and convey by every means the total impact and communication. The manifesto is challenging, and it would be false not to admit that one could more easily write his own poem than so thoroughly submerge his activity to the mind of another, especially since part of the communication or part of the manner will remain uncongenial to the translator, however much he may admire his author. We can only hope that our product has not fallen too short of the goal we set ourselves.

The solution we propose for the grandmother paradox will be reserved for its proper place in the essays. Since such difficulties are common in the Pindaric text, we obviously cannot deal with them in the preparatory essays as difficulties, but must gloss them over; the solution must appear as though there had been no problem at all but merely a self-evident step or item in the counterpoised parts of the entire poem. It was, moreover, our desire to relieve Pindar of the incrustations of centuries of misinterpretation, and it seemed best, therefore, for the most part (we could not always restrain ourselves) to pretend that the accumulation of wrong ideas had never existed. And yet the scholar may be disconcerted sometimes to find an interpretation so much at variance with the present consensus of opinion. We invite him to examine the evidence that is presented in a more academic manner in one of the translator's essays in *Hermes* and in his forthcoming *Marginalia Pindarica*.

And yet as long as Jourdainese is practiced in the classroom, these translations will sound strange to those who "know" Greek. But even if the translations have failed as poetry, they may yet accomplish a twofold benefit. Perhaps they will entice a few more to attempt the study of the Greek

language —for Pindar is certainly poetry in the original—
and perhaps the demonstration to the classicist that his daily
exercise has warped his sensitivity will elicit new methods
for training these new students. Hopefully, when Greek
speaks directly to the reader, it will say to him different
things.

PYTHIA IV: And Orpheus Journeyed

To move from Homer to Pindar involves an even greater change than that implied by a span of three centuries: the drastic evolutions which must attend the transition from the heroic age to the early fifth century; from epic, orally, perhaps spontaneously, composed for an illiterate people by an illiterate poet, to the daedal, written lyric that eulogized members of the new Enlightenment. Pindar's patrons, to be sure, looked to the past; it was from the mythological genealogies that they traced their divine right to rule. And Pindar himself, the Theban whose city had Medized, faced the world of developing Athenian democracy with apprehension and nostalgia. The Pindaric tone results from the poet's often futile attempt to see alive again the ancient gods, to clothe his aristocrats in the raiment of Homer: a glorious futility, for although the aristocrat himself may not realize the potential of his position, Pindar will teach him, will pass from external splendor, from victory and wealth, to a metaphysical significance, the resurgence of past ideals. The victor thought, no doubt, only of the contest and of the renown. Pindar will show, as well, the responsibility.

The epic's aim was didactic: to recall, as best one could, historical events and thereby define the Greeks as a people distinct amid an alien ethnic context. If the past were to be forgotten, the Greek as Greek would disappear. The exigencies of oral composition entail, of course, much more than mere recollection. The simple memorable event becomes a theme on which innumerable variations are played; the poet is judged for his virtuosity, for his skill in obscuring the germinal unity of his theme beneath the baroque elegance of his ornamentation. It would be an error in interpretation to attempt to extract the unity of an Homeric poem and to base one's critical evaluation upon the success of the endeavor. The correct aesthetic *assumes* the unity and appreciates primarily the diversity.

Although the Pindaric ode is written literature, it, like the epic, was composed for oral presentation or performance; this is an observation of greater significance than is at first apparent. The ode may have been written, but it was not read, or at least not read in the same way that we read books for enjoyment today. The ode was the libretto, a mnemonic device; in performance it came alive to music and dance. In written form it was a monument, like an inscription or, indeed, an engraving in gold —the honor accorded "Olympia VII" by its patron. The performance of the ode placed it in the same context as the contemporary rhapsodic recitations of the Homeric poems. Not only were such recitations still current; the poems themselves were the basis of a Greek's education. To be sure, their original simple didactic purpose had been reinterpreted amid the welter of new ideas that thinkers and poets, as well as the demands of advanced civilization, had brought into vogue. Homer, a secular Bible, was searched for confirmation; it too was made to offer comment on problems alien to its original composition. The new thought, furthermore, was expressed largely in the very formulae of Homer's language. The obscurity of Heraclitus, for example, results from his attempt to write a mnemonically memorable prose that uses mythological language, for lack of the vocabulary necessary for his new thought; Heraclitus no doubt could not himself conceive his ideas in a form clearer than that allowed by his place in the Greek cultural continuum. Or, we might ask, was Xenophanes poet or philosopher? For the Greek, there was no dichotomy. Homer, Hesiod, Xenophanes, Heraclitus —they all told you the truth, or a truth. One memorized Homer; one thought with his language. The audience could hear the commonplace, like the popular song that was the cantus firmus of an early Renaissance parody-mass. We might say that Pindar was a Bach who could not only play countless and complex variations on a simple melody, but did so for an audience which could still, at times, indulge in the Renaissance dances from which the melody sprang. One would not ask, was that a saraband? —of course it was! What else could it be? One paid attention to what was *made* of the saraband.

Pindar's audience, therefore, could respond directly to the ornamentation. The translator, however, presents the ode to a reader necessarily deficient in the formulae of archaic Greek poetry and the clichés of the epinician ode. The ode seems formless; Pindar intended a dazzling display of brilliance, a lavishness he could afford, because his poem, like the Homeric epic, grew from a unified conception. If we attempt to extricate the unity of an ode, we are doing no less than repeating the error of Aristotle. Aristotle came after the great age of Greek literature and, more important, after the transition from oral to written literature had been fully accomplished. For an artist of his time, the problem of creation was one of reducing multiform reality to an aesthetic whole. The process is the exact opposite of that in the archaic age: from unity, the event which alone could be remembered, to multiform variations. The Aristotelian thought-process gathers numerous examples, then expects to abstract the universal; but it is only an age that reads and has recorded details that can afford the luxury of such a process. When Aristotle turns his attention to previous literature, he is struck by the occurrence of unity. But why not? Of course, that is a saraband. The translators must, therefore, confess to a certain reluctance in presenting a uniform plan for their ode, for this is not the task of the critic of archaic Greek literature. We will speak of the unity merely as a prelude, to supply the deficiency in the contemporary reader, who must then be prepared for the arabesques which "meaning motion fan fresh our wits with wonder."

Pindar's "Pythia IV," like Homer's *Odyssey,* elaborates the theme of homecoming, the *nostos,* and the theme of hospitality, *xenia,* the kindness shown a Greek wanderer away from home. The poem begins with the statement of the theme: "This day visit a friend's house," the palace of Arcesilaos, king of Cyrene, the victor celebrated in this ode; it ends with the idea restated: the ode is the gift of hospitality given to Arcesilaos' banished kinsman, Damophilos, when he visited Pindar at Thebes:

> . . . . what welling stream
> He found but recently—this poem for gods—
> The Theban's hospitality.

The ode selects for its myth a scene from the homeward journey of Medea and the Argonauts. Euphamos, the destined founder of the Battid line, in which Arcesilaos is the eighth, receives at Libya a divine sign of *xenia,* a piece of Africa in token of his descendants' future possession of that continent:

> And then it was this deity, alone, did come to us,
> A holy man, it seemed, with radiance
> In his face. The words he spoke were friendly —
> The greeting of a host who meets his guests as they arrive .
> Inviting them to banquet entertainment.

With a startling change, however, this episode becomes only the prelude to a more extended narration, the journey out to

Phasis, the expedition which changed the name of the Black
Sea from Hostile, in Greek, to the Euxine, the Sea of Hospitality. This well-known story is only tangentially broached,
but it forms the armature for the main part of the ode:

> . . . . the relentless frenzy
> Of the Colliding Rocks —two of them, and both alive:
>   whirling
> Whorls, more vortex-like than rank
> On rank of rumbling winds. But today no longer:
> For the passage of the demigods put
> An end to them.

The journey out is preceded by the return of Jason to his
father's mansions and his sinister meeting with his relative,
Pelias, who had usurped the realm from Jason's family. Pelias'
greeting is a cruel perversion of the Homeric formula to welcome a wandering traveler, the usual preliminary to the
offer of *xenia*:

> . . . . "What land, traveler,
>   Do you claim for country? What groundling
>   Got you from a hag's grey womb?
>   Come now, speak it out! Don't defile a noble
>   Family! None of your odious lies!"

This signal lack of hospitality is compensated for by the joy
of Aeson, Jason's father:

> . . . . He entered the house and his father knew him:
> His eyes gushed tears that welled
> From aged lids, for now his spirit
> Within him quickened and he rejoiced at the sight of a son
>   select
> And handsome beyond all men.

The scene is obviously a short version of the cliché "the meeting of father and son," which had been elaborated more fully

at the close of the *Odyssey*. Jason's relatives arrive, the lyric equivalent of Homer's catalog of ships:

> . . . . And then to banquet:
> With words of sweet friendship Jason received them all,
> Contriving appropriate gifts of hospitality,
> And prolonged all manner of good cheer
> For five whole days and nights together, culling
> The rare and sacred flower of well-being.

There is, in chronological order, a feigned reconciliation with Pelias, followed by the journey out to Phasis. The pattern is repeated. Aeëtes, king of the Colchians, is hostile, or at least refuses to surrender the Golden Fleece without subjecting Jason to a contest, which incidentally provides a mythological archetype to Arcesilaos' victory at Pytho, the ostensible occasion of this ode. Medea, like Aeson and the kinsmen, counteracts her father's cruelty by a lavish show of hospitality: she falls in love with Jason and provides the poet with an opportunity to describe that weird love-charm contrived by Aphrodite, the wryneck, a woodpecker of sorts, fastened to a whirling wheel. The bird's torment binds the lover with its cry:

> Then Lady of the Poignant Arrows brought
> From Olympos the dappled wryneck pinioned spread-eagled,
>   bird
> Bound fast to its prison wheel —
> Such was the origin: the Cypriote goddess
> Had given mankind that wingèd madness . . .

Medea's witchcraft is her gift of hospitality:

> . . . . the woman
> Had admitted him to the knowledge of her drugs.

The poem ends with a major variation, the *nostos* and *xenia* themes combined: we shall have occasion to speak of this later.

Eight forms of the word *xenia* appear amidst the elaborations and the ode itself ends with the last word of the sphragistic close, again a grammatical transformation of the same
Greek root. The other events of the narration present reminiscences of the major theme. The yearning of the crew for
the Argo, for example, consecrates the triad: comradeship,
danger, excellence:

> None would stay by his mother's side, digesting gruel—
> Life devoid of danger;
> But at the risk of death would find with others of his age
> That finest catalyst for his excellence.

The lines recall, of course, the choice which faced Achilles.
Jason's sojourn with Chiron not only saves him as a child from
the furies of Pelias and provides him with the traditional
heroic beast-man education (Achilles and Asclepios came
from the same school), but also recalls the myth of Ixion, who
slept with a cloud —his punishment from Zeus for a signal
breach of the laws of host and guest in attempting to seduce
Hera: Centaur was the child of that union, and his children
by Magnesian mares became the race of centaurs. For us,
the allusion is centrifugal; for the Greek, just the opposite: it
bears with it all the comfort and security of the familiar re-
lating with the familiar. The Greek aesthetic experience was
basically one of recognition, of hearing what one already
knew, but in a form calculated to avoid boredom. "Let me
tell you something you already know," as Jason says to Pelias.

Battos journeys to Delphi, where he seeks a cure for his
stuttering. The priestess greets him instead with surprising
hospitality as the future founder of Libya, the founder of
the line which is to flourish eight generations later in the rule
of Arcesilaos of Cyrene. Battos himself is seventeen generations after Euphamos, who sailed on the ship Argo and who
bedded with Lemnian women on the return trip. This episode presents a reconciliation of a kind: the women had
previously murdered all the males on the island, and now in
receiving the Argonauts they provide a home away from

home and consent again to the domination of the male principle. Their hospitality incidentally forms an opposite parallel to the hostile reception the Argonauts had received at Phasis, signaled by the recurrence of the Greek verb "to mingle, to mix," which may have a sexual significance. They are, moreover, an instance of the poem's recurrent plant-image:

And they slept with them—that foreign plowland
Which (what day? what nights?) received the seed destined
For the sunburst of this, your abundance.
For the race of Euphamos had there been planted, thence
To time has waxed eternal.

It is from this stock that Arcesilaos has grown:

> Today no less—
> Spring, call it, crimson flowers at their height—
> Arcesilaos, eighth of his line, flourishes in sons.

Colonization, itself a form of homecoming, particularly when such homecoming has been predestined, lends itself easily to this image. Libya, the nymph who becomes a continent ("This city of victory's chariot/ Upon the gleaming breast of Africa"), will "plant/ Her root in the country where Zeus-Ammon is established"; the plant will grow into the cities of Arcesilaos' realm. Indeed, Euphamos receives as the sign of his line's predestined colonization of Africa a clod of Libyan plowland. If he had preserved this piece of Africa, his descendants, his Lacedaemonian heirs from his native city of Taenaron, in the fourth generation would have taken that continent; instead, as the Argonauts approach Thera, the clod is washed overboard ("Look: here at this island vast Libya's/ Potent seed is prematurely/ Spilled!"); the result is the historically realized event: Euphamos' Lemnian descendants, after a longer delay, seventeen generations, join with the Lacedaemonians of the Dorian tribal movements at the time of Battos: "To bring cities in ships/ To the fertile tract of Nile." Euphamos' clod of earth suffers a minor transmutation into the furrows cut by Jason's plow at Phasis, as he drives

the fire-breathing bulls. The image is recalled also in the reconciliation speech of Jason and Pelias, when he retells their
common ancestry from Enarea (the heifer), the mother of
Cretheus and Salmoneus:

> . . . . we,
> Who now see this golden force,
> This sun, were sown in her third generation.

Jason consents to relinquish the lands of his parents, provided only he be given the rights of monarchy:

> . . . . The flocks, therefore,
> I relinquish and the russet herds of cattle and the farmlands
> Of my parents, all their acreage
> In your possession earning you fat profits.

The fragments reunite in the gigantic fugue-like culmi-
nation of the last two triads, where the themes of *xenia* and
nostos and the plant-image are introduced in the form of an
Oedipos-riddle: Will the king be bright enough to understand the teaching of the ode?

> . . . . should someone
> Strip the branches off
> A great oak-tree, should sharp axe shame
> The wonder and the beauty of its form;
> Defoliated, it would nonetheless elect to offer its credentials
> For review: let it meet its end in a winter fire—no matter!
> Or standing, one amongst the upright
> Pillars in a lord's mansion, propped
> In alien walls, let it serve in its tedious task,
> Desolate, deprived of its native land.

The oak-tree now is Damophilos, whom Arcesilaos had banished from Cyrene, since he had, apparently, led a political
faction against the king. It was Damophilos who commissioned this ode, as a gift for Arcesilaos to celebrate his triumph; the ode would normally be sung back home in Cyrene,

at a banquet honoring the Pythian victory. ("Pythia V" was the ode commissioned by Arcesilaos himself.) In this setting, the ode gives voice to the exile's plea: hospitality, *xenia, nostos*, the exile's return:

. . . . Hear his prayer: to have done with his disease, to drain
To the dregs his cup,
See his home
One day, to banquet by Apollo's spring: may
He again surrender to the joy of youth; with statesman
Connoisseurs, hold high
His exquisite lyre, touch
A concord.

Arcesilaos must heal the disease ("Your gentle hand/ Lay on; minister as you must to the ulcerating wound"); the image of illness and cure has grown from the knowledge of Chiron, who taught Asclepios, and from the magic drugs of Medea. The laying-on of hands is apposite to Arcesilaos, for his kingdom of Libya is the mythological child of that Epaphos who was born of Io by the touch of Zeus. The lyric poet, speaking perhaps in person at the banquet, presents Damophilos as the poet of civil concord; the lyre that Pindar holds becomes the sign of political peace. The cup that Damophilos will drain to the dregs is the cup of his affliction which, if his prayer is heard, will become the cup from which he will drink at Arcesilaos' celebration: the victory celebration has turned into welcome for the exile returned. Whether the prayer was heard or not is unknown. There is, in any case, perhaps some justification in seeing a connection between Damophilos' banishment and the political upheavals which a few years after the date of this poem (462 B.C.) were to cost Arcesilaos his life.

———

For Homer, mere narration was didactic; it recalled history. What we appreciate in Homer's art was the natural result of

25

a virtuoso poet's attempt to clothe the remembered historical event with the appearance of diversity. Pindar, however, has selected and marshalled the events of his narration so that they point up a teaching not necessarily inherent in history; that is to say, history is now not the content of thought but its subject and its material. Perhaps this was the only procedure to be expected from a poet or a people who were trained to see the constantly receding past as relevant to the present, a past whose teaching, accepted at face value, became increasingly anachronistic. Arcesilaos is shown that his own family history, as it is retold in the words of Pindar, counsels him to accept back his banished kinsman, Damophilos. For those of our contemporaries who find great art universal, this is certainly a disappointment in Pindar's ode. However, the translators might confess that in all good will they have never faced the problems of Macbeth, or Hamlet, or Othello, or, yet, King Lear. It is the strangeness of great literature, its *alien* quality, which helps wrench us from the complacence of the contemporary monochrome.

The archaic mind of Homer, as it attempts to elaborate the unified idea, has recourse to digression within digression. The structure that results is that of the ring-composition: in simplest form, this might be represented by the formula ABCBA. Thus the *Iliad* begins with the funeral pyres of the Greeks as they suffer under the plague sent by Apollo, and ends with the pyre of Hector. Other events are similarly balanced at the beginning and end. When Herodotus, a later contemporary of Pindar, comes to write the prose history of the Persian wars, he still, perhaps unconsciously, structures the history on the basis of digressions, although this time linearly directed: ABCBADE etc. This is to say that in the fifth century, the natural patterns of oral composition were still operative: literature was still orally presented and therefore conceived for oral presentation. It is not surprising, in view of this, that Pindar's ode is conceived in ring-composition.

Pythia IV

The first section of the poem is framed by the mention of the Delphic victory of Arcesilaos:

With Arcesilaos in his revels heighten
The wind of song, my Muse, the debt we owe
To Leto's children and to Pytho, (11. 3-5)
. . . .
. . . . Today no less —
Spring, call it, crimson flowers at their height—
Arcesilaos, eighth of his line, flourishes in sons.
Apollo and Pytho and the Delphic
Overseers gave him the glory
Of the race-course: and I shall celebrate him, the debt we
    owe the Muses; (11. 91-96)

The recurrence of the idea (after an interval of three triads) that the victory is a debt Pindar owes clearly marks the second section as an elaboration of the introductory idea; the largest cycle is completed and the expectation in the listener's mind is that the poem is near its close. Indeed, much of the traditional matter for the epinician song has been treated, and the ode should end. Pindar, however, plays structure against structure, defies the cliché, and introduces, in subordinate grammatical position, the new subject of the ode:

. . . . and I shall celebrate him, the debt we owe the Muses,
Celebrate the ram's pure Golden Fleece.

In parody of the Homeric epic's opening, the new narration is launched, fulfillment, now realized, of the opening lines "heighten/ The wind of song":

What first cause engaged them,
The motive for the voyage? What challenge fixed its steel
    strong
Rivets? A prophecy. . . .

The story that follows makes "Pythia IV" the longest of Pindar's odes, nearly three times the average length—

Damophilos' ostentatious bribe for his return. This section is not completed until just before the final fugue-like tree-riddle:

> . . . . and Leto's son
> Bestowed on you the plains of Libya
> To magnify, respected of the gods—and a city to govern, divine
> Cyrene, enthroned in golden state.

It will be interesting to observe how the events are arranged within the first Arcesilaos ring-structure. We have seen that the narrative plateaus develop as variations and ornamentations of the idea which formed the ode's didactic purpose; the technique of the actual narration within the units is determined by another counterpoised organizing force. Pindar ordinarily adopts a tangential approach to the events narrated, describing the lesser aspects, the concomitant details rather than the main line of the plot; and thereby he succeeds in preserving the presentational brilliance of lyric poetry without succumbing unduly to the discursive elements in narration. In "Pythia IV" the central idea of prophecy, which evolves quite naturally from the commemoration of a victory at Apollo's Delphic sanctuary and from the particular role this prophetic shrine had played in the family history of Arcesilaos, becomes the armature upon which are built the successive stages of the narration. Prophecy is uniquely suited for the tangential treatment of plot, for it contains, within its enigmatic statement, indications of future as well as present time, a natural disruption of normal chronology. The events are arranged in simple recessive chronological units. The victory of Arcesilaos is historically the most recent and begins the ode. The Delphic prophecy which is given to Battos is eight generations before Arcesilaos (roughly 630 B.C.). This prophecy, the fulfillment of which will produce the kingdom of Arcesilaos, is itself the fulfillment of a prophecy made in the mythological past, seventeen generations earlier than Battos: Medea's prophecy delivered at Thera, which also relates to the founding of Libya. Her pronouncement is the interpretation of an omen which the Argonauts witnessed a few days earlier as they left the coast of Africa and Triton's estuary. The god Eurypylos had given Euphamos a token of his line's future monarchical rights to Libya. Medea mentions that this omen occurred just after the Argonauts' twelve-day journey over the African desert; it therefore comprises the most historically remote event in this section of the ode. The structure is now completed by the same events in reverse order, that is to say, chronological order; the poet displays his brilliance by elaborating each repeated event so that it now appears in fuller color. For example, the prophecy delivered to Battos appears first in the reverse series:

Where once the ministrant of Zeus and his golden eagles —
As it happened, Apollo himself was then in residence—
    prophesied
Battos would be the holy founder
Of fruit-bearing Libya: that he would leave
His sacred island to colonize this city of victory's chariot
Upon the gleaming breast of Africa.

This statement reappears toward the end of the cycle:

Phoebos in his gold rich mansion
Will manifest to him the ordinance (down
He had gone to Pytho's temple) to bring cities in ships
To the fertile tract of Nile,
Cronos' son.
. . . .
Blessed, o son of Polymnastos! You are this story's subject —
It was you exalted by the Bee of Delphi,
Whose spontaneous outcry was your oracle.
Thrice she greeted you: Rejoice! Thrice hailed you
Destined to become Cyrene's king,
When you had put the question merely: Could the gods cure
Your stuttering speech?

In graphic form, the ring-structure may be represented as follows. (The line references are included merely to show the relative length and placement of the episodes.)

Time

A (1-5)   Victory of Arcesilaos at Delphi
B (6-11) Delphic prophecy given to Battos,
                 ancestor of Arcesilaos
C (12-27) Medea's prophecy delivered at Thera,
                 relative to the founding of Libya
D (28-35) Omen at Lake Triton
E (36-39) Reference to the twelve-day African
                 overland journey
D (40-53) Omen at Lake Triton
C (53-76) Narrative of the loss of the clod:
                 (60-71) Hypothetical result
                 (72-76) Actual result
B (76-90) Delphic prophecy given to Battos,
                 ancestor of Arcesilaos
A (91-96) Victory of Arcesilaos at Delphi

The second section, as has been noted, begins with the epic questions. There is a marked shift in technique. The narration is now more leisurely expanded in the Homeric manner and follows a chronological arrangement. Full attention is focused on discreet units, and the smooth flow of narration is broken by time-leaps from plateau to plateau: the arrival of Jason in Iolcos and his first interview with the king, the reconciliation scene, the departure of the Argonauts, the founding of an altar to Poseidon at the mouth of the Pontos, the passage of the Argo through the Symplagades, and the events at Colchis. This simple narrative line, however, supports various excursions into past history: Jason's education in Chiron's cave; Jason's birth and his parents' ruse to preserve him from harm by Pelias; Phrixos and the previous history of the Golden Fleece (one might even say that the translation of Phrixos' remains constitutes an additional variant of the exile's return); and the various summary statements about the genealogies or previous lives of the heroes who joined Jason for the sailing of the Argo. The central idea of prophecy still provides the armature, the pretext for tangential narration. Jason's arrival at Iolcos had already been predicted to Pelias at Delphi; and Phrixos himself had on another occasion appeared to Pelias in a dream, demanding the return of the Golden Fleece; and again at Delphi, Pelias had apparently received confirmation of his dream. Prophecy is operative also in the description of the Argonauts as they take to sea from Iolcos; and in the exotic land of Colchis, prophecy in the form of magic becomes the order of the day, with Aphrodite's wryneck bird, Medea's ointments, and the fire-breathing bulls.

Pindar displays his virtuosity by again interrupting the narrative with an elaboration of a break-off formula, an additional variation of the *nostos* theme: time presses and the poet must now take a shorter path, for the poem not only tells of the trip of the first ship, the Argo, but is itself a journey, an image vaguely suggested at the poem's beginning: "the wind of song":

> Too long for me to travel by chariot the highway home:
> Time presses.
> And there's a certain short cut
> That I know: I blaze for others the trail of poetry.

The short cut is a diametrically different style of poetry. Narrative material is greatly compressed: in two strophes, a résumé of events, from the killing of the serpent which guarded the Golden Fleece, up to the present generation of Arcesilaos, touches lightly upon the Lemnian women, Medea's murder of Pelias, and the colonization of Libya from the island of Thera. The accelerated time-sequence merely reverses the similar span of twenty-five generations which is comprised in the first sentence of the ode.

The prophecy-armature becomes an additional voice in the final fugue. For a riddle is a kind of prophecy: both hide the truth in enigmatic language which is often not understood until the event is at hand. To solve this puzzle, the king will need the wisdom of Oedipos. Damophilos is its answer; his reinstatement will make Pindar's own prophecy of political peace true. The journey must pass on into the future:

> .... Time passes,
> The wind falls, sails are changed
> For new.

The ode's journey is ending. May blessèd Cyrene have the guidance of a god, a sudden pilot for its kings; the image passes effortlessly into that commonest of ancient images, the ship of state.

————

Orpheus, father of poets, journeyed to Phasis as one of the Argonauts:

> And Apollo's own, there came the lyre player, father
> Of song, richly lauded Orpheus.

His presence was essential. Archaic man defined himself as an exterior; he was no more or less than what others thought him to be. The glory of the expedition would have been wasted, or indeed could not have existed, without the poet—the man who had words in his power, the man who knew the formulaic language which made events memorable and could transmit them to posterity. Jason receives the athlete's crown, "leaves of greenery," but the honor is not complete until his life has passed into song. Arcesilaos could not be content merely with the powers of kingship. His life was nothing unless he lived in the eyes of others. To compete oneself in the Greek "national" games, contests which could trace their foundations back to the acts of gods, or even to compete by proxy, to enter a team of four from a noble stable, as in the present case, gave the aristocrat of Pindar's day the same challenge that Pelias offers Jason in the quest for the Golden Fleece: honor, all golden, that can be won if you are good enough, the opportunity to teach your contemporaries *come l'uom s'etterna*. Kingship was not enough; all the heroes of old were kings. How did man become god?

As the oral epic grows from unity, a hero reduced to

his essential, and therefore memorable, dimension multiplies into other heroes who share some element with their stereotype. The poet of course attempts to obscure their common parentage; he will give the illusion of diversity. Thus the *Odyssey* will tell of the homecoming of Odysseus as a multiform of the homecoming of Agamemnon, Menelaos, and the other heroes. Penelope is merely the opposite, the mirror-fugue, of the faithless wife, Clytemnestra. The net in Aeschylus' *Oresteia* in which Clytemnestra ensnares her husband is the same piece of weaving, transmuted, that occupied the long years of Penelope's lonely vigil. The murderous bath is the same bath which a good host offers his traveling friend to welcome him to his house; even Clytemnestra, in the *Choephoroe*, must attempt to offer this gesture to the disguised Orestes, although of course her own past makes the welcome sinister. The audience, capable of reciting parts of the Homeric poems, had been conditioned unconsciously from childhood to this mode of thought. The contemporary who became the subject of song became as well, in their minds and in his own, for a moment at least, the ancient hero. The poet therefore was essential. In his hands were the keys to immortality. Victory at Pytho, the Delphic sanctuary, places, as Pindar says, a debt upon the poet. He must not only celebrate the rebirth of ancient divinity, but he must do so in a manner worthy of Orpheus, for thus he too becomes a hero. Pindar, in this ode, which is seen as a poetic journey, is himself again the Argonauts' Orpheus. Just as Orpheus travels as an equal of demigods, so Pindar will refuse a place inferior to his Jason, Arcesilaos.

We have said that archaic man was external; this is no doubt true for Arcesilaos. Pindar, who had seen the nobles of his native city side with the Persian invaders, who had seen them ignominiously defeated and considered traitors to Greece, must have come to realize that the shining splendor of gold, the external sign, could not alone define. When the external was dishonored, it had no reservoir of hidden respect: how could such glory have vanished? He will attempt then to see that which passes show. He will not, of course, make the leap to internal definition: he could not, and this very inability, conditioned by his place in the Greek cultural development, is what produces the tremendous power and beauty of his poetry. He must use the external to define the internal; he must make the show signify; he must struggle with his patron to make the phenomenon a reliable witness to the man Pindar demands to see. The poet has a debt to pay. The patron has the responsibility of being worthy of that debt. It is not surprising that the content of his poetry outstrips its communicative value; perhaps this is what produces poetry. He would come close to Hopkins' profession of faith:

> The world is charged with the grandeur of God.
>   It will flame out, like shining from shook foil;
>   It gathers to a greatness, like the ooze of oil
> Crushed.

The wealth of Apollo's "gold-rich mansion" was not weighed as bullion. The Delphic sanctuary was abundant in gold and bronze fashioned by artists and craftsmen into commemorative statuary and dedicatory gifts to the god. Gold was art, was beauty, was the proof of the external, and the therefore only possible honor accorded divinity: Apollo was patron of the games: could gold in the aristocrat's hand signify as much? Apollo was patron of the lyre: could the poetry that Pindar sang equal the centuries of accumulated wealth deposited in the temple? Apollo was moreover the particular patron of Arcesilaos' family: could the king be worthy of this trust? Could god be manifest?

In the virtuosity of his poetry, Pindar surpasses the physical excellence of the performing athlete. Indeed, the games did not make clear distinction between athletic ability and the grace of music and dance. Not victory alone sufficed, but it was the beauty of an artist performing in the perfection of his nature. Pindar's poetry is the extreme development of the past tradition. The pressures of the new age are there, but they merely force the poet to find still greater significance in the past. Perhaps he had gone too far: his contemporaries apparently found him sometimes too difficult to understand. His was the final flourishing of the archaic mind; his contemporary, Aeschylus, has much in common with him, but the dramatist was an Athenian and his vision was of an evolving cosmos that would find completion in the developing greatness of Athens, the democratic state. What Pindar wanted to say could not yet be said; when the language was found, it was too late. The *Characters* of Theophrastus and the psychological studies of Aristotle describe more clearly the soul of man, but the burden of communication had by that time passed to prose. The king was politician: he was not poet; he was not the ancient god.

The genealogy of the family of Jason. The names in parentheses are not mentioned in the poem.

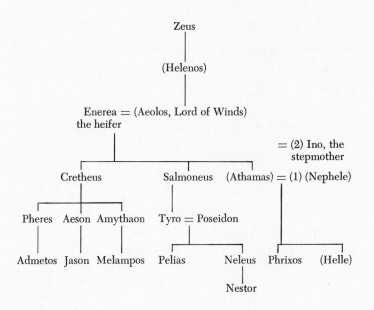

Pythia IV: For Arcesilaos, King of Cyrene: Victory With Chariot

---

ΣΑΜΕΡΟΝ ΜΕΝ ΧΡΗ ΣΕ ΠΑΡ ΑΝΔΡΙ ΦΙΛΩΙ

STROPHE

This day visit a friend's house:
Attend Cyrene's king, in the land where horses graze:
With Arcesilaos in his revels heighten
The wind of song, my Muse, the debt we owe
To Leto's children and to Pytho,
Where once the ministrant of Zeus and his golden eagles —
As it happened, Apollo himself was then in residence—
    prophesied
Battos would be the holy founder
Of fruit-bearing Libya: that he would leave
His sacred island to colonize this city of victory's chariot
Upon the gleaming breast of Africa,

ANTISTROPHE

And thus would bring to pass, at a remove
Of seventeen generations, the prediction which once Medea,
    mantic

Pythia IV

Daughter of Aeëtes, uttered
At Thera, inspired message from immortal mouth —
That princess of the Colchians. These words
She spoke to captain Jason's crew of demigods:
"Hear me, sons of gods and of men stout-hearted: I say
That from this land that breaks the sea
Epaphos' daughter will one day plant
Her root in the country where Zeus-Ammon is established:
    men's care
Will make it flourish forth in cities.

EPODE

When once finned dolphins' wings have been exchanged
For horses swift,
And oars for reins,
Then will they drive the whirlwind racing chariot.
Great cities shall claim Thera for their mother —
The omen thus accomplished
That once at Triton's estuary
A god in human form presented, a gift of earth
In pledge of hospitality: Euphamos disembarked to claim it,
And thunder of Cronian Zeus the Father
Ratified the sign.

STROPHE

The anchor bite of bronze had just
Been weighed —swift Argo's bridle— when he appeared.
(Twelve days' portage
From Ocean, we had borne the hull across
The desert back of earth:
For I had counseled that the ship be drawn up on the land.)
And then it was this deity, alone, did come to us,
A holy man, it seemed, with radiance
In his face. The words he spoke were friendly —
The greeting of a host who meets his guests as they arrive
Inviting them to banquet entertainment.

37

ANTISTROPHE

But our homeward journey beckoned with delight
Anticipated: we could not stay. He introduced himself:
    Eurypylos,
Son of Earth's immortal
Mover; accepted our excuse; but nonetheless would try
To give a token of his friendship,
Whatever was at hand: he snatched a clod of plowland.
Our hero declined it not but leaped ashore; his hand
Clasped the other's hand and Euphamos
Received miraculous sod. This earth
Now is overboard, they tell me, washed by the waves away:
It goes floating on the westward current,

EPODE

Pursuing the waters of the evening sea. And this despite
The caution I urged
On the men delegated
To guard it close —but their minds wandered, neglectful!
Look: here at this island vast Libya's
Potent seed is prematurely
Spilled! I mean that had
He cast the clod in the cave that leads to Hades, back home
In his holy Taenaron —King Euphamos, son
Of Poseidon Hipparch and Tityos' daughter,
Europa, who bore him

STROPHE

On the banks of Cephisos— then would his blood,
In the children of the fourth generation, have taken that wide
    continent
With Danaeans, when they rise up
Out of great Lacedaemon and the gulf of Argos
And Mycenae to go forth and colonize.
This will not be: but he has bedded with foreign
Women and in them will he find his chosen people who,

38

I foresee, will come with gods' mark
To this island and beget a man to be lord
Of the plains and the black rain clouds. In time to come,
Phoebos in his gold rich mansion

ANTISTROPHE

Will manifest to him the ordinance (down
He had gone to Pytho's temple) to bring cities in ships
To the fertile tract of Nile,
Cronos' son." Thus Medea's chapter
And her verse: transfixed, silent,
The heroes, peers of gods, heard revelation.
Blessed, o son of Polymnastos! You are this story's subject —
It was you exalted by the Bee of Delphi,
Whose spontaneous outcry was your oracle.
Thrice she greeted you: Rejoice! Thrice hailed you
Destined to become Cyrene's king,

EPODE

When you had put the question merely: Could the gods cure
Your stuttering speech?
Today no less —
Spring, call it, crimson flowers at their height—
Arcesilaos, eighth of his line, flourishes in sons.
Apollo and Pytho and the Delphic
Overseers gave him the glory
Of the race-course: and I shall celebrate him, the debt we
    owe the Muses;
Celebrate the ram's pure Golden Fleece: the gods
Planted honor for the Minyans when they
Set sail.

STROPHE

What first cause engaged them,
The motive for the voyage? What challenge fixed its steel
    strong
Rivets? A prophecy: Pelias

39

Would die by the illustrious Aeolids —murdered outright
Or victim of relentless machinations;
It came to him, an oracle pronounced at the Navel-stone
Of timbered Mother Earth, and chilled his devious heart:
"Beware the man who wears one
Sandal! Keep constant watch
Should ever he come from sheer upland pastures down
To the clear air of historic Iolcos—

ANTISTROPHE

A traveler, perhaps, or citizen." And come
At last he did, a giant of a man with a pair of spears;
He wore both styles
Of clothing: Magnesia's native costume clung
To the shape of his wondrous limbs,
And a leopard-skin was cover against the icy rains;
A splendid mane of hair unshorn went flowing
Down his whole back, blazing.
He did not stop but strode straight on
To the market-place, stood there unperturbed, and tried his
     wits just
At the time when business has reached its height.

EPODE

None knew him, but despite their awe, one of the number,
Conjecturing, said:
"He's not Apollo,
Is he? Nor Aphrodite's husband, the bronze chariot's
Driver. And Iphimedeia's sons are dead, they say,
Died on glistening Naxos —
Otos and you, brave
Lord Epialtes. Nor Tityos: Artemis plucked from her quiver
Invincible the wind-swift arrow and hunted him down —
Men must content their aspirations only
With women of their rank."

Pythia IV

While they were exchanging such remarks
Out loud, Pelias, in a wagon made of planks and drawn by
    mules
At break-neck speed came
Driving up. He was dumbfounded! He focused on
That single sandal in plain
View, the man's right foot! He hid
His fear —to gain information: "What land, traveler,
Do you claim for country? What groundling
Got you from a hag's grey womb?
Come now, speak it out! Don't defile a noble
Family! None of your odious lies!"

ANTISTROPHE

He met the challenge with words of mildness
And thus replied: "I say —and time will bear me out—
That I am Chiron's pupil.
From his cave I come, from Chariclo's and Philyra's, where
    those saintly
Daughters of Centaur raised me.
My twenty years are ended —for no act of mine
Nor word amiss did they complain— and here have I come
Home, escorting from its exile my father's
Ancient kingship, those dignities hereditary,
Now perverted, which once, in time past, Zeus
Conferred on the Lord Aeolos and his sons.

EPODE

I say 'perverted,' for I have learned that Pelias, the lawless
Lily-livered usurper,
Violently stripped
My parents of their ancient royal rights legitimate:
No sooner had I seen the light of day, than they,
Fearing the excess of their master's

Arrogance, set up a wailing
In the house —dark, feigned funeral— and amidst the
    women's
Lamentations, sent me in my purple swaddling-clothes
    (by stealth:
Night shared my road) to be raised
By Cronian Chiron.

STROPHE

But enough of that: you know the main
Points. Show me, you loyal citizens, the way to my fathers'
Mansion, its splendor and white
Horses. For I am no stranger but Aeson's son
Come home to my native country;
That holy creature called me by the name of Jason."
Thus he spoke. He entered the house and his father knew
    him:
His eyes gushed tears that welled
From aged lids, for now his spirit
Within him quickened and he rejoiced at the sight of a son
    select
And handsome beyond all men.

ANTISTROPHE

And Aeson's brothers, both of them, came
When they had news of the arrival: Pheres set out from
    Hypereis,
His spring not far distant;
From Messana journeyed Amythaon. Shortly thereafter
Arrived Admetos and Melampos,
Eager to welcome their cousin. And then to banquet:
With words of sweet friendship Jason received them all,
Contriving appropriate gifts of hospitality,
And prolonged all manner of good cheer
For five whole days and nights together, culling
The rare and sacred flower of well-being.

Pythia IV

But on the sixth, he set before them serious fare
And confided to his kinsmen
His story from the beginning.
They approved his plan, rose when he leaped up
From his couch and went with him to the court of Pelias.
They rushed in and took their stand,
Were announced, and Pelias in person
Met them, the son of Tyro, who bore love in her hair.
Drops of mildness fell in Jason's voice
And laid the groundwork for reconciliation: "Scion
Of Poseidon of the Rock,

The human mind would sooner choose
A crooked profit than simple justice, even though a rough
Day-after lies ahead;
But we must, you and I, discipline our passions
And for the future weave prosperity.
Let me tell you something you already know: one
Heifer was the mother of Cretheus and audacious Salmoneus;
    we,
Who now see this golden force,
This sun, were sown in her third generation.
The Destinies that apportion our lot turn away when families
    feud
And honor is hidden, propriety forgotten.

We would be wrong, dividing by the sword's
Bronze blade or the hurled spear our ancestors' great
Legacy. The flocks, therefore,
I relinquish and the russet herds of cattle and the farmlands
Of my parents, all their acreage
In your possession earning you fat profits:
It matters little that I am overly solicitous for your estate.
But the scepter of monarchy and the throne where once

43

Cretheus' son, ensconced, meted out
Straight justice for his nation of horsemen —these things
    (and let
There be no grievance shared between us)

EPODE

Surrender to me, or else your kingship may provoke
Fresh troubles."
Those were his words,
And Pelias calmly answered: "I shall do as you say.
However. . . . Life's final age attends me
Now; in you, youth's
Flower seethes: you
Can appease the dead man's wrath. Phrixos commands that
    someone
Fetch his remains and bring from the mansions of Aeëtes
The deep fleece, the ram's skin
Whereon he was saved

STROPHE

From the sea and the unholy arrows of his step-mother.
A wondrous dream haunts me, keeps uttering this
    supplication;
I have consulted the oracle at Castalia
Whether I should pursue the matter: she urges me post-haste
To equip a naval expedition.
Would you be willing to undertake this feat? And I
Swear to cede to you all royal pomp and power —
A firm pledge: may the Zeus of our fathers
Be witness to us both." The terms were accepted,
The covenant approved; they separated. And Jason, for his
    part,
Lost no time in dispatching heralds

ANTISTROPHE

To make the proclamation everywhere that his ship
Was taking on a crew. Thereupon there came three whom
    battle

Pythia IV

Never wearied, sons
Of Cronian Zeus by Leda and Alcmene (for the fluttering
Of her eyelashes!); and two with a crest
Of hair, men of the Earth-Shaker's line, who honored
Valor, one out of Pylos, the other from Cape Taenaron:
Their glory came to pass, that of Euphamos and yours,
O Periclymenos (and wide was your force felt).
And Apollo's own, there came the lyre player, father
Of song, richly lauded Orpheus.

EPODE

And Hermes of the golden staff sent his pair of sons
On this boundless venture,
Echion —they both
Clamored in boisterous youth— and Erytos. And swift
They came, those dwellers from the pedestal of Mount
    Pangaeos:
Swift, for heartily, with laughter,
He rushed them on: the King of the Winds,
Father Boreas decked out Zetes and Calaïs, men —
But their backs both bristled with crimson wings.
A sweet and all-persuasive yearning for the good
Ship Argo

STROPHE

Hera kindled in those godly peers:
None would stay by his mother's side, digesting gruel —
Life devoid of danger;
But at the risk of death would find with others of his age
That finest catalyst for his excellence.
When into Iolcos they sailed, this flowering of seamen,
Jason counted them all and approved what he saw. Next
His priest, by birds of prophecy and the cast
Of magic lots, launched the expedition:
For Mopsos had found the auguries propitious. Over the
    beaked
Prow now they hung the anchors;

ANTISTROPHE

And holding in his hands a patera of gold,
The captain at the stern invoked the father of heaven's
    hierarchy,
Zeus of the lightning's lance,
And the swift beat of the waves' ways, and the winds,
Nights, and the paths of the sea,
Days of gladness, and the longed-for voyage home.
From out the clouds resounded the auspicious sound of
    thunder;
And a coruscating flash of brilliance, the bolt
Came in answer bursting forth.
The tension broke; the heroes drew easier breath, trusting
In the signs of god. Their herald, the seer,

EPODE

Bid them lean to the oars, for the omens assured their hopes
A sweet fulfillment.
And the rowing that ensued
Issued insatiate, swift from the movement of their hands.
With an escort of South Wind, they came to the mouth of the
    Hostile
Sea: there they established
Ocean Poseidon's sanctuary;
A russet herd of Thracian bulls they found at hand,
And the palmate hollow of a fresh-cut altar stone.
As they thrust themselves into the depths of danger,
They prayed the Lord

STROPHE

Of Ships for deliverance from the relentless frenzy
Of the Colliding Rocks —two of them, and both alive:
    whirling
Whorls, more vortex-like than rank
On rank of rumbling winds. But today no longer:
For the passage of the demigods put

An end to them. And then —to Phasis, where
They joined full-force in battle with the dark-skinned
    Colchians
And Aeëtes himself took the field.
Then Lady of the Poignant Arrows brought
From Olympos the dappled wryneck pinioned spread-eagled,
    bird
Bound fast to its prison wheel —

ANTISTROPHE

Such was the origin: the Cypriote goddess
Had given mankind that wingèd madness and taught
    Aesonides
The lore of spells and charms,
Whereby he might corrupt Medea to forget her filial
Piety: that her love be Greece,
Her mind afire, reeling beneath Infatuation's
Lash. She proceeded to disclose the trial of strength her
    father
Meant to set; in an unguent-base she compounded
Antidotes to counteract the pain and gave
It him to anoint himself. And they pledged each their troth
To join and share the delights of marriage.

EPODE

Aeëtes was the obstacle: he dragged in their midst the
    plowshare hard
As steel and the oxen
Whose tawny maws
Burning breathed forth flames of fire;
Their hoofs of bronze beat the earth they trod on.
Single-handed he led them to the yoke
And drove the furrow down
Straight, splitting a fathom deep the turfy back
Of earth. He challenged: "There's your work: let the king —
The captain of your ship— do it and earn
That Ageless Pallet —

STROPHE

I mean the Fleece with flashing gold
Fringe." He had spoken; then Jason threw off his saffron cloak
And attacked the work, placing
His trust in god. The fire could not swerve him: for the
woman
Had admitted him to the knowledge of her drugs.
He wrenched the plowshare, bound the oxen's necks
Forcibly to the gear, applied to their muscular flanks the goad
Ever relentless: that man of strength
Finished full measure the task
Assigned. A howl —Aeëtes', amazed at Jason's ability:
Grief had robbed him of power to speak.

ANTISTROPHE

But in salutation his comrades stretched their hands
Toward the masterful man, crowned him with the victor's
wreath —
Leaves of greenery—, and embraced him
With sweet speech. The Sun's astounding son,
Aeëtes, cut them short:
He told them where it was the knife of Phrixos flayed
The shining fleece. (Little hope that Jason survive this
labor!)
For it lay in a dragon's lair, clenched
In jaws infuriate —the beast from tip
To tail surpassed the mass of a fifty-oared ship
Built by the blows of iron tools.

EPODE

Too long for me to travel by chariot the highway home:
Time presses.
And there's a certain short cut
That I know: I blaze for others the trail of poetry.
He killed by craft the steel-eyed serpent iridescent
Coiling, and stole, O Arcesilaos,
With her consent Medea —murderer

Of Pelias. They mingled with Ocean's waters and the Red Sea
And at Lemnos the tribe of self-made widows; and there
In games they showed the prowess of their limbs:
Raiment was the prize.

STROPHE

And they slept with them —that foreign plowland
Which (what day? what nights?) received the seed destined
For the sunburst of this, your abundance.
For the race of Euphamos had there been planted, thence
To time has waxed eternal.
With people of Lacedaemon's stock commingled, they sometime
Later colonized the isle of Thera, Callista most lovely.
They rose from there, and Leto's son
Bestowed on you the plains of Libya
To magnify, respected of the gods —and a city to govern, divine
Cyrene, enthroned in golden state;

ANTISTROPHE

Here you have devised all righteousness of policy.
Be an Oedipos now and try your hand at riddles: should someone
Strip the branches off
A great oak-tree, should sharp axe shame
The wonder and the beauty of its form;
Defoliated, it would nonetheless elect to offer its credentials
For review: let it meet its end in a winter fire —no matter!
Or standing, one amongst the upright
Pillars in a lord's mansion, propped
In alien walls, let it serve in its tedious task,
Desolate, deprived of its native land.

EPODE

You are the very doctor that is needed, you the luminary
Paean dignifies:

Your gentle hand
Lay on; minister as you must to the ulcerating wound.
To shake the city down is easy even
For the weak; to set it in its place
Again —a hard task
To wrestle with, unless a god be sudden pilot for its kings.
The Graces weave you in their tapestry. Up, courage!
Devote your whole attention to the cares
Of blessèd Cyrene.

STROPHE

Heed too this phrase from Homer;
Apply it to your case: That messenger is best, he says, who
    brings
The most prestige to all he does;
No less is magnified my Muse by forthright message.
Cyrene has known —and the renownèd
Court of Battos— the wisdom of Damophilos, his justice.
For he is young, a man of the new generation; nonetheless in
    council
An elder statesman, one who has seen
The full century span of life;
He robs the slanderous tongue of its tinsel voice; has learned
To hate a citizen aspiring too high;

ANTISTROPHE

Leads no faction against the nobles;
Nor protracts enactment of a matter: no, for the crucial
    moment
In human concerns is of brief
Duration; he recognized it, was its squire, and not its drudge
Attendant. No greater pain
Than this: to know what's needed, yet perforce,
As they say, "to have one's foot abroad." A veritable Atlas,
He wrestles with the sky, far now
From the fatherland, far from his proper estate.

Pythia IV

Zeus the Immortal freed the Titans. Time passes,
The wind falls, sails are changed

EPODE

For new. Hear his prayer: to have done with his disease, to
  drain
To the dregs his cup,
See his home
One day, to banquet by Apollo's spring: may
He again surrender to the joy of youth; with statesman
Connoisseurs, hold high
His exquisite lyre, touch
A concord: cause no trouble, expect none from the city.
And he would tell you, Arcesilaos, what welling stream
He found but recently —this poem for gods—
The Theban's hospitality.

OLYMPIA VII: The Life of the Metaphor

The opening flourish of Pindar's ode to Diagoras of Rhodes is not experience poetically coded, it is rather the experience itself.

The splendor of the scene inspired the famous ode of Ronsard (and does it vibrate in the background of Mallarmé's *"Rien, cette écume, vierge vers"*?). The father of the bride presents the toast to his son-in-law; Pindar offers the gift of the Muses, poured nectar. The balanced correspondence is demanded by the remnants of the archaic simile-structure and by the antistrophic responsion: the kinesthetic experience of music and dance makes the poet's toast a mirror of the father's gesture, but it would be vain to press too closely the terms of the comparison. Who, for example, is the bride? And the opulent hand? Surely this is not to be seen as a metaphor for the Muse's inspiration.

The Homeric simile perceives a point of comparison between one thing and another; the first term of the comparison, however, will experience an extended elaboration quite independent of the basis of comparison; the linear movement of the narration is suspended for a moment while the poet indulges his audience's appreciation for agréments. The early lyric poets maintain the archaic structure: Sappho, for example, compares a woman's beauty to the moon, which shines among the lesser stars; the moonlight and night then receive autonomous description with no further reference back to the point of departure. We have come, of course, full circle: our contemporary poets have taught us again the beauty of this form. A good part of the magnificence —and the difficulty— of Saint-John Perse, for example, stems from a procedure in which independent variations are played upon an original perception, perhaps never stated.

Pindar's simile grows from the epic tradition, but, unlike Dante, Pindar is not consciously archaizing. His similes show the pressures of the new age: he is thinking with the modes and structures of thought at his disposal. Although the toast begins in the poet's mind as a simple Homeric adornment (he salutes the victor as the father honors the groom), the poetic reality of the gesture will assume a life of its own in the development of the ode. Just as Mallarmé's poem does not stand for the toast but actually accompanies the raising of the glass, so also Pindar's ode is part of the symposium ceremony; his audience, the assembled guests, will recognize themselves. The ornament is a multiform of the present scene and as such it will become the dominant idea in the composition of the poem.

Marriage and festival begin and close the cycle which comprises the poem's life:

> .... when celebrate the sons of Eratos,
> All the city is festival.

This statement not only returns to the opening scene of the ode, but also in a sense summarizes the extended significance that the private celebration of Diagoras and his kinsmen has undergone in the course of the poem. The victor's ancestry and the story of Tlepolemos and his murder of Licymnios form merely a bridge to the proto-history of the island of Rhodes itself. The fact that the people of Lindos inscribed this ode in letters of gold in their temple indicates that a wider public accepted the national significance of Pindar's hymn. There was indeed no blood connection between the line of Tlepolemos and the aboriginal inhabitants of the island, the Heliads, or the Sun's children. And yet the connection is abruptly made: Pindar will celebrate Diagoras by telling of the marriage of the Sun and Rhodes:

> And now these sounds accompany. Diagoras and I leave
>   ship; I sing
> Of the sea-child, Aphrodite's daughter
> And the Sun's bride, Rhodes.

It will be toward this major mythic treatment of the marriage theme that the poem progresses. This event is the most remote historically of the narrated episodes. The poet, in the archaic manner, moves retrogressively.

Diagoras is praised; his island home is mentioned; the fact that Rhodes is an Argive fortress (perhaps a reference to its precarious position off-shore a hostile Persia) requires an explanation: how the people of Tiryns colonized the three-citied island under the leadership of Tlepolemos. This migration was the Delphic oracle's penance prescribed to Tlepolemos for his murder of Licymnios. But this is all transition. It was at Rhodes that Athena had been born from the head of Zeus; it was here that the golden snow had fallen. This, too, is transition, for it leads to the Sun's injunction that his children perpetually commemorate the birth with festival and ceremony. The Sun is of course interested, since the island of Rhodes is his bride, his portion received in the allotment of the realms of Heaven and Earth. It is that narration, the birth and marriage of Rhodes, which closes the cycle begun in the first epode:

> She sprouted from the wet salt wave —
> His island holding— his, who fathers the trenchant
>   sunburst rays,
> And chariots the fire his horses
> Breathe. He slept with his Rhodes, ...

The poem now moves chronologically forward again. The Sun's sons founded the three cities of the island. It was to this island that Tlepolemos came from Tiryns. It delights the deified Tlepolemos to see his Diagoras victorious. An extensive list of Diagoras' victories (he was the foremost boxer of his day) balances the cursory mention, in the first epode, of his crowning achievements, his triumphs at Olympia and Pytho.

It can be seen that the archaic ring-structure is operative in the poem's conception. The rings sometimes overlap, however, and the organizing principle can perhaps be more clearly seen in the way the opening simile, a poetic figure which has assumed the force of an actual experience, dominates the composition.

The wedding banquet is, of course, suggestive of the marriage of the Sun and Rhodes. It is also not unrelated to the motif of birth, however, especially since the birth of Rhodes coincides with her marriage to the Sun; the birth of Athena presents a repetition of the same mythic type. In a broader sense, the opening simile is a ceremony or festival, and the festival motif reappears in the rites which the Sun enjoined on his people to commemorate the birth of Athena; it also suggests the ceremonies honoring Tlepolemos at Rhodes, a brief mention which is used as a bridge to return to the list of Diagoras' victories:

Tlepolemos, who led the colonists from Tiryns,
Is a god
Commemorated: procession and aroma of sheep sacrificed;
    the games,
The decision, whose flowers crowned
Diagoras twice.

The poem itself is presented at a festival and comprises the poet's own ceremony to the patron of Olympia:

    .... O Zeus, our Father,
    Who lord the ridge

Of Atabyrios, we tender you formalities of Olympic
Ode.

"Olympia VII" thus offers multiforms of itself.

Tlepolemos had murdered Licymnios —an embarrassing
event in a family chronicle. But *le pire n'est pas toujours sûr,*
as Claudel subtitles his *Soulier de satin:* murder, *etiam pec-
cata,* is sometimes a blessing. Without his momentary de-
rangement ("Upheavals of the mind/ Derange the wisest"),
Rhodes would not have been founded. The motif of the alternation of good and bad or good *from* bad grows also from
the opening simile. The father's toast: οἴκοθεν οἴκαδε, "From my
house to yours," perhaps connotes the idea, "My loss is your
gain." But we need not press this point too far, for the simile
ends with a variation on the commonplace that glory is transitory:

> . . . . rich
> The man whom fame possesses.
> On one, now another, this grace of life
> Its abundance visits —
> The singing lyre, the counterpoint of flutes.

It will be this idea which pervades the entire poem.

The mythic material repeatedly illustrates the emergence of festival from error. The Sun's injunction to his people to perform burnt sacrifice to the newborn Athena was
erroneously observed: they forgot to bring fire with them
when they climbed to the Acropolis. The sentence in Greek,
the approximate center of the poem, turns around; the un-
usual placement of the negative at the end of the sentence
turns success into failure: καὶ τοὶ γὰρ αἰθοίσας ἔχοντες σπέρμ' ἀνέ-
βαν φλογὸς οὔ: "Now, did they take up embers? a spark of fire?
No!" But Zeus accepted their flameless rites and showered
the city with golden snow; Athena granted them mastery in
the arts. The birth of Rhodes also is preceded by error: in the
allotment of territories, the Sun, who was absent, was forgot-

ten; in lieu of reapportionment, he accepted the surfacing island of Rhodes as his realm. Tlepolemos too found good from bad:

> Here from bitterness was sweet deliverance: here
> Tlepolemos, who led the colonists from Tiryns,
> Is a god
> Commemorated.

It is this success which justifies the poet's claim "to relate, correct, authenticate" the history of the Tlepolemids, a history known from the Homeric catalog of ships (B 653-670). The Homeric passage relates the same events but does not so clearly show the emergence of success from Tlepolemos' error; the golden snow is perhaps only tangentially referred to at the end of the Homeric passage: καί σφιν θεσπέσιον πλοῦτον κατέχενε Κρονίων: "And Cronian showered them with riches." Pindar completes his amplification of the Homeric passage by a return to the idea of correction; he now claims to have done what he intended: "Is not the poet/ Who's informed the greater for his truth?" There is no need to see a reference here to the Telchines, the aboriginal Rhodians predating the Heliads. Pindar is not correcting some misty rumor about the magic arts of these unnamed people; the position of the passage at the end of the Homeric exegesis clearly marks it as a variation of the opening claim to correct the emphasis in the epic, and therefore supposedly authentic, source; σοφία has its normal Pindaric meaning of poetic art.

The mythic material is punctuated by recurrent returns to variations played upon the gnomic idea of vicissitude or reversal of fortune.

> . . . . Numberless the errors
> That throng man's
> Mind: no way to find
> What present choice is best for future time.

This is Pindar's comment that introduces the murder of Licymnios. The same idea occurs in the narration of the com-
memoratory-sacrifice mistake:

> . . . . Reverence
> But Forethought, and the joy in perfection falls ours:
> Ah, but mists of oblivion spread, obliterate
> The landmarks: from the straightaway of action our minds
> Stray.

Forethought is the Greek name for Prometheus; his mention
in this context is ominous, since everyone knew his punishment for the theft of fire; the Pindaric passage plays against
a second reversal myth. Our translation prints the recurrent
variations in italics. The reader will notice how predominant
the idea is and how varied the modes by which it is introduced and expressed.

The themes of festival and vicissitude combine in the
closing epode:

> Temper the grace you grant:
> Let countrymen and foreigner know
> The path he walks shuns excess: the inspiration
> Of his noble line has taught him
> Well. Show forth the seed
> Of Callianax: when celebrate the sons of Eratos
> All the city is festival.
> Yes, but a single moment in time and the winds
> Wheel round, kindled here, now there.

It would be extraneous to see here a reference to the supposed difficult position of Rhodian aristocrats on a democratic
Rhodes belonging to the Athenian Confederacy. The passage
is a commonplace of the epinician ode. The poet does not
want to overpraise the hero, for it is a well-known observation
that the great (mountains, trees, men) are worn away by the
forces of nature. Pindar presents the poetic conceit in a bril-

liant variation. Zeus, patron of the Olympic games, is asked to grant Diagoras a moderate spirit; this request has evolved from the dazzling list of the victor's triumphs—surely enough to lead the ordinary man astray. But Diagoras is not that kind of person; even though his victory is a national festival, he is aware, as the poet reminds him, that all is transitory. Mythic material and gnomic utterance intensify what the athlete already knows. Was this the meaning of the earlier emphasis on vicissitude? Has Pindar, in composing his ode for an extraordinary athlete, woven this conceit into the entire fabric of his poem? *Le pire n'est pas toujours sûr* means for Claudel (and St. Augustine) that God sometimes writes straight in crooked lines. Pindar's cosmos has no such beneficent deity. Greatness must be won but the heights of success are precarious. *Le pire n'est pas toujours sûr* implies for Pindar the corollary: *le mieux n'est pas toujours sûr.*

The poem refuses to be satisfied by any simple formulation of its structure. One part reflects another; transition becomes major theme; the meaning grows, expands. The simile becomes the poem, which becomes the conceit, which becomes the poem. And so on. The chart attempts to summarize what cannot be summarized. It will be seen that the center of the poem is the correction of the Homeric tradition. The birth-marriage of Rhodes, however, is also suffused with the epic aura: it is included within a larger circle which encompasses the correction-section: the mention of the three-citied state of Rhodes, which perhaps grows as an amplification of the Homeric line (B 656: Λίνδον Ἰηλυσόν τε καὶ ἀργινόεντα Κάμειρον: "Lindos, Ialysos, and chalk-white Camiros"). The cycle of the marriage of the Sun and Rhodes and the cycle of Tlepolemos both spread beyond the central nucleus of Homeric exegesis. The poem is several pebbles scattered in water; each has its own universe, each relates with the others. Was the structure conscious? Probably not. Conscious art is more perfect (one thinks of the Latin poets ...) and less beautiful.

Pindar's was a mind that took centuries to prepare; the poem is the reverberation of contemporaneity as it works with the gift of the past.

The simile has progressed beyond the Homeric stage; it has become an actual event and grown into an ode.

Lines		Description
1-17	*	Marriage simile
	*	. . . . . victories of Diagoras
18-19		Marriage of Sun and Rhodes
20-24		Victories of Diagoras
25-26		Rhodes: three-citied state
27		CORRECTION OF THE TRADITION (EXEGESIS OF HOMER B 653-670)
28-46	*	Tlepolemos
46-47		Golden snow
48-66	*	Birth of Athena
66-72		Golden snow and Athena's gifts
73		CORRECTION OF TRADITION
74-97		Allotment: birth and marriage of Rhodes
98-104		Rhodes: three-citied state
105-109		Tlepolemos
109-121		Victories of Diagoras
120-130	*	The marriage simile realized

*Means the occurrence of the gnomic variations on vicissitude.

Line references refer to the translation and are included merely to show the relative length of the sections; note, for example, that the speed of the retrogressive narration is much greater than the chronological return. Tlepolemos, however, is longer in the first narration than in the second. The poem is not therefore lopsided: the birth of Athena is its mathematical center, but the birth of Rhodes is the point toward which it is directed. Would such balance have been clearer in choreographic presentation?

OLYMPIA VII: For Diagoras of Rhodes: Victory in Boxing

ΦΙΑΛΑΝ ΩΣ ΕΙ ΤΙΣ ΑΦΝΕΑΣ ΑΠΟ ΧΕΙΡΟΣ ΕΛΩΝ

STROPHE

A chalice in opulent hand let someone take
(Within foams a dew of vine):
And proffer
To the young man, his son-in-law, the toast: *From my house*
to yours. All

Of gold, this crest of wealth,
This banquet elegance to honor his new
Alliance, exalt him
To the envy of the guests for his consenting bride.

ANTISTROPHE

And I no less libation of nectar, this gift
Of Muses, pour, my mind's fruit
Delectable,
Propitiation to the victors' triumph at Pytho and Olympia:
rich

The man whom fame possesses.
On one, now another, this grace of life
Its abundance visits —
The singing lyre, the counterpoint of flutes.

EPODE

And now these sounds accompany. Diagoras and I leave ship;
    I sing
Of the sea-child, Aphrodite's daughter
And the Sun's bride, Rhodes:
A fair-fought victory, this man colossal, crowned
At the Alpheos River (Poetry:
The boxer's payment) and at the spring
Castalia —him and his father shall I celebrate,
Damagetos, beloved of Justice:
Offshore vast dancing Asia's promontory,
Their triple-citied island state is Argive fortress.

STROPHE

Hear my intention: to relate, correct, authenticate,
From that first Tlepolemos, their common history:
Heracles'
Race and its wide dominions. On the father's side, they glory
In descent from Zeus, these Amyntorids,
Whose mother was Astydameia. *Numberless the errors*
That throng man's
Mind: no way to find

ANTISTROPHE

What present choice is best for future time.
Witness Alcmene's bastard brother
Murdered:
Licymnios was slain at Tiryns as he left the Midean court:
A staff of solid olive-wood
And the wrathful hand of this island's founder.
(*Upheavals of the mind*
Derange the wisest.) He consulted the oracle.

Olympia VII

The answer from the incensed temple sanctum: that deity
    whose hair is gold
Spoke of sailing: from Cape
Lerne straight to these meadows
In the sea: here once the god of gods had rained
On the city snow all gold
When down from the crown of his head
Leaped (Hephaestos was midwife with axe
Of beaten bronze) the daughter
Athena: her loud, long shout of jubilation
Made Heaven quake and mother Earth.

STROPHE

And then divinity of light upon us, Hyperion's
Son, enjoined on his elect perpetual
Commemoration:
Be they the first to found an altar monstrance to the goddess
And consecrate burnt offering:
Thus exults the Father's heart and his daughter
Of the thunder-spear! *Reverence*
But Forethought, and the joy in perfection falls ours:

ANTISTROPHE

Ah, but mists of oblivion spread, obliterate
The landmarks: from the straightaway of action our minds
Stray.
Now, did they take up embers? a spark of fire? No!
The Acropolis rites were flameless,
But the sanctuary nonetheless auspicious: there gathered
An ochre cloud —
Zeus' goldenfall. And the Owl-Goddess —the arts

EPODE

Were her endowment. Their master craftsman hands
    surpassed all here on earth
(The statues that lined their roads

Were alive almost and moving)
And deep were they embued in glory. Is not the poet
Who's informed the greater for his truth?
When Zeus and the Immortals were dividing up
The land —so says an ancient legend—
Rhodes was not yet here
And nowhere to be seen on the ocean's sea; she lay
An island hidden deep at the bottom of the brine.

STROPHE

Now, in his absence, the Sun was left without
His share allotted (all forgot this god
Of holiness).
He came petitioning and Zeus would move for
        reapportionment, but "No!"
He said, "Down through the grey
Water turbulence I see her burgeoning,
Rising —land!
Where man will nobly pasture flocks.

ANTISTROPHE

Have cast the lot, my Lachesis (gold girds your forehead):
Pledge by the gods' most solemn oath
Incontrovertible;
Second the will of Cronian Zeus: into the shining air
Her crest shall surface, henceforth
To be my guerdon." The summit of his hopes fell
True, accomplished:
She sprouted from the wet salt wave —

EPODE

His island holding— his, who fathers the trenchant sunburst
        rays,
And chariots the fire his horses
Breathe. He slept with his Rhodes,
Begot seven sons, passed on to these
Alone of their contemporaries the highest
Knowledge. And one begot

Ialysos, his first-born, and Camiros and Lindos.
Apart, each held a third,
His share of the divided patrimony —estates and cities:
Three royal seats bore each its ruler's name.

STROPHE

Here from bitterness was sweet deliverance: here
Tlepolemos, who led the colonists from Tiryns,
Is a god
Commemorated: procession and aroma of sheep sacrificed;
    the games,
The decision, whose flowers crowned
Diagoras twice. Then at the honored Isthmian
Four times successful;
Once at Nemea, and again; and on the rock

ANTISTROPHE

Of Athens; and at Argos: bronze recognition, the shield;
And Arcadia: trophies; Thebes; the traditional
Boeotian
Contests; Pellene; and Aegina: six triumphs there; at Megara
The graven stones know
No other name. O Zeus, our Father,
Who lord the ridge
Of Atabyrios, we tender you formalities of Olympic

EPODE

Ode: receive them and the victor whose fists found him his
    finest hour;
Temper the grace you grant:
Let countrymen and foreigner know
The path he walks shuns excess: the inspiration
Of his noble line has taught him
Well. Show forth the seed
Of Callianax: when celebrate the sons of Eratos,
All the city is festival.
Yes, but a single moment in time and the winds
Wheel round, kindled here, now there.

Nemea VI: The Parentage of Gods and Men

For Pindar to declare the common origin of gods and men from their mother Earth startles only our own contemporaries, who find their religious, or atheistic, orientation within the Judao-Christian context. The gulf between human and divine for us is qualitative. The attributes of divinity, however, had to be discovered, and at no point in the development was god very far in advance of man's ability to conceptualize him. The ancient god was just one step higher in the hierarchy established on earth. Zeus is Agamemnon's superior, just as Agamemnon is superior to Thersites. "Sin," or hybris, is an act of violence which attempts to transgress the barriers of the Establishment. Agamemnon can kill Thersites, or his own peers, but he must do vassalage to his lord. For Thersites to speak out of turn is sin; for Agamemnon to challenge the deity is sin. God is stronger than man, but he differs only quantitatively in his lusts or his abilities. It is one of the great beauties of the Homeric poems that the divine plane of action merely ornaments the human. Achilles is Zeus-like and Zeus is like Achilles. They have the same narrative connotations, and the plan of Achilles to withdraw from battle so that the Greeks may suffer is also the plan of Zeus, and is accomplished. Golden Chryses is angered, and there is plague because Apollo the Golden is angered and sends the plague. When a god speaks to man, the voice comes not from afar. Achilles, who has no name for himself, no definition of himself other than "Achilles," the reputation-complex which exists only in the eyes of others, must explain his actions as a conflict of opposed organs in his body; his heart may tell him to do one thing, while his diaphragm opposes —or the impulse may come from a god's voice —a god who had his origin in the attributes of human heroism and therefore presents no alien motivation. Helen reluctantly obeys Aphrodite, that most beautiful of goddesses; she goes to the bed of Paris, but could Helen, the most beautiful of women, really have done otherwise?

When god differs from man, he is merely the mirror-image of the human: man is mortal and dies: god is immortal and does not die. The earlier gods, of course, did die, and this new attribute of divinity produces an embarrassing paradox. Where are Ouranos and Cronos, the predecessors of Zeus? How, too, could Pausanias visit the grave of the immortal Zeus? Even in a story as well known as the Aeschylean *Prometheus*, Zeus must gain the secret of Prometheus if he is to endure. It is significant that immortality, that is to say, the paramount attribute of deity, is defined as the negation of a human attribute.

When man evolves a new society, standards of human behavior change. A democracy requires a principle of balance and fairness, and Zeus, too, will be redefined as a cosmic moral principle; his action will be confined now within the limits of human law and the god will be expected to offer the new code his divine sanction. The common man no less will demand a share in the good things of this world and the next; god is now the savior, the liberator, the natural man of the *Bacchae*. When man defines himself as the spirit which escapes the body and the restraints of life in society, god, too, is this same freed spirit. Sin, likewise, must keep step with the development; when the Establishment has lost authority, hybris can no longer be the crime of social mobility but will seek new definitions in the moral sphere. It will be a long time, however, before man in the Greek tradition may sin in thought alone. Socrates will attempt to end the dichotomy between the newly discovered individual self and the socially conditioned morality —the well-known *nomos-physis* controversy of the fifth century—by finding the soul of man to be but the microcosm of the established order, that is to say, by finding that *physis* is after all nothing but *nomos*. The natural man is also the moral man, if he but realize it. Socrates' god, the daemonion, is the superego, the internalized moral education of society which speaks as his voice of conscience. This daemonion is a tremendous move forward, but in another sense it merely realizes the implications of the Homeric man-god relationship. The Christian god, who developed, unlike the Greek gods, within a codified priestly tradition, cannot so gracefully at once forget and resume his past. Christ, the new god, is only part of divinity, the son of God the Father, on whose left hand sits the Divine Spirit.

Pindar begins his poem for Alcimidas of Aegina by recalling the Hesiodic tradition, the common origin of gods and men, but unlike Hesiod, who is silent on this point, he attempts to explain why these brothers differ. In the cosmic game that is our life, the gods, by virtue of their surpassing strength, always come off the victors; their prize is the brazen heaven that endures forever, the Homeric formulae that describe their habitation. Yet it is possible that in some games man, too, may perform brilliantly: the athlete in the national Games or the poet in his high paedeutic function as transmitter and interpreter of the tradition. It is in "Nemea VI" that we see most clearly why a great poet concerned himself with athletic contests. He and the athlete are dual manifestations of the same resurgence and proof of divinity.

Greek thought dealt with serious problems before the

Greek language had evolved the syntax and vocabulary appropriate to them. The magnificence of Greek poetry is caused in part by its ability to discuss our adult problems in the language we knew before we conceptualized. In Greek, philosophy speaks to us with the language that we forgot when we became children. Hesiod narrates the union of Sky and Earth —in our language, but not in his, the confrontation of matter and force. The rain fecundates the earth and the Great Mother produces offspring. The harvest is sometimes gods, sometimes mere men, sometimes heroes or god-like men. In Alcimidas' line, Pindar sees proof of this alternation. His grandfather was Praxidamas, who in 544 B.C. was the first Aeginetan victor at Olympia; Alcimidas' great-grandfather, Saocleides, like Alcimidas' own father, was undistinguished, but his great-great-grandfather, Hagesimachos, had also been an athlete of distinction. Why is a good bloodline not always good? Pindar seeks the answer in the earth-metaphor:

> . . . behold his stock
> Is as the fields in tillage bearing harvest where lean years
> Follow fat: the plains' gift sometimes is abundance,
> Life for us a twelvemonth;
> Sometimes fallow they rest and hoard their energy.

The land in this generation has again been fertile. But the athlete must realize the potential inherent in his physical endowment: what he is must be translated into action if he is to be what he is and what Zeus ordains. He is a hunter and his quarry is himself.

The poet here finds his function. The victor's family has passed into history, and history is in the poet's trust:

> . . . . for men pass on,
> But the singer
> And the song escort from oblivion the beauty that was theirs.

The poet now becomes the plowman who sows the seed which will produce the hero, when, through the poem, he grows eternal to time.

The poet in the poet's mind is seen as a double of the image-complex that surrounds Alcimidas. This is to say that unconsciously he feels himself attracted into the same poetic aura that he has established for the athlete. The house of Alcimidas is a storehouse of prizes won at the contests. The poet, perhaps elaborating the Homeric formula ἔπεα πτερόεντα ("winged words")— an epithet he uses for song himself in "Isthmia V"— becomes an athlete, the archer whose words will strike the target, the exact truth, which will neither fall short of the just amount of praise nor soar too high beyond reality. This conceit is, of course, one of the clichés of the epinician ode, but in this poem, it is particularly apposite; for, as the archer, he, like Alcimidas, is the huntsman. Alcimidas seeks his own potential; he must realize in action who he is that others may know him:

> He is come from lovely Nemea, from the games, where
> This boy contested, tracking down what Zeus ordains —
> Endowment now made
> Manifest: there in the arena he was a huntsman
> Treading step by step in the footprints of his family . . .

The same verb (μεθέπων) occurs when the poet comes to speak of his own relation to the past tradition and the present poetic task. He has, of course, helped the athlete find himself by showing him again his own family; he has oriented him by reference to the past. But this recording of the past is but part of the poet's paedeutic function. Great men provide the poet with the poet's potential, the theme that the poet will realize in writing his ode. There are many narratives that glorify the island of Aegina, many avenues of praise. He can choose from the epic material, the account of the battle of Achilles and Memnon, which was told in the lost *Aithiopis* of Arctinos of Miletos. The ancient poet's words were winged and his poem leapt the sea to Ethiopia. Perhaps Pindar is thinking of the tradition in which Memnon's companions at Troy were changed to birds who mourned their king's death, while each dawn the drops of dew that fell were tears that his mother shed. Pindar cuts short his retelling of this story, however, and thereby reduces to a minimum the mythic section of the ode.

The break-off formula repeats the avenue-image:

> .... That was the royal road those
> Who went before me found: I myself now follow it
> And care for it my melody.

He, like the athlete, orients the present by the past, but the epic theme is less fertile for the poem that he is writing; it is the great man whom he has seen himself that excites his enthusiasm:

> And yet it is the nearest wave, swirling at the ship's rudder —
> As they say— that ever sets a maelstrom in our desire.

Pindar has summarily related the epic theme, the death of Memnon; but it is in the present that he, as huntsman, finds the seed with which to sow the field where the Pierides plough:

> So, willingly, I track down this double burden for my
>   back;
> I step forth,
> A herald to clarion this five and twentieth
> Proclamation, victory in the Games whose epithets are
>   sacred.

Does Pindar mean that in the poet's tendance the Earth-Mother again produces a hero, that is to say, the man who, like Achilles, is the subject of song and the peer of gods? The great man acts, he performs in the contests; but is it in the poet's virtuosity that the original division between the brothers, man and god, can to some extent be breached? Certainly this is the meaning of the passage. We cannot agree with Professor Norwood that Pindar is groaning under the weight of the family archives, a programme imposed by an oppressively prideful patron. The "double burden" is the past and the present, Achilles and Alcimidas. Perhaps ἄχθος, the burden, means the theme, the "burden" or song that is the base in melodic elaboration.

But Alcimidas is only a boy and his victory is at a minor game. The poet has shown him the example of Praxidamas and his kinsmen; he has shown him Achilles, who through his father, Peleus, son of Aeacos, was an Aeginetan. He has shown Alcimidas what it was that the athlete was seeking in the arena. Victory at Olympia, that choice crown, is what Zeus ordains. The rest is in the trainer's hands:

> But to the dolphin in its swiftness through the sea I would
>   liken
> Melesias, the reinsman
> Of your limbs and strength.

Another match may reverse the decision that kept Alcimidas from the Flowers of Olympia.

The ending of the poem is abrupt, but not insufficient. It is a cliché of the ode that a victory at a minor game should lead to greater achievement. The poem is open to the future. It might not, however, be too fanciful to see particular significance in the comparison of the famous Athenian trainer, Melesias, to the dolphin. The image has of course been latent in earlier sections of the poem. The victor's house is a ship laden with a cargo of encomia. The wave at the ship's rudder is the poet's phrase which he borrows from the language of proverbs to refer to the victor, Alcimidas. Bury may be right in linking the poet and Melesias, and seeing a pun in the poet's "melody" (μελέτη—"care," probably as a technical term for poetic theme) and Melesias (Μελησίας). The dolphin, for the Greeks, had too its narrative connotations in poetry, and that mammal's melomanic propensities had become common mythic material in the story of the poet, Arion, who was saved from the sea on the dolphin's back. Past and present are the poet's melodies. In Melesias' keeping will be the future greatness that Alcimidas has yet to realize, but both poet and trainer are essential to teach the young man.

The poem defies our attempt to translate it into a rational "philosophical" exposition. It could not have been conceived in the poet's mind on the conceptual level and then clothed in the raiment of poetry (the most obvious example of such a procedure is the narrative-poetic trappings with which Bunyan clothed Christian dogma in his *Pilgrim's Progress*). The poem is itself its only complete expression. It lives only by that most complex interaction of image played upon image, of "idea" or vision imposed upon or emerging from the past tradition. The poet's "wisdom" or σοφία entails not only his mastery of the formulae and clichés of his craft, the mythical-historical narratives, but also his ability, at least in the case of a poet as great as Pindar, to think completely within the syntactic patterns of *poetic* communication.

Are we justified in seeing the complex and reciprocal interactions of poet and athlete mirrored in the basic structure or thought-pattern of this ode? In its simplest form, we might see a progression from games to poet to athlete back to poet and games. Each step and each return bears with it not only the power of language borrowed from a rich tradition but also the intensity gained by its own reverberations in its new context. In seeking the significance of the Hesiodic genealogy, the poet's thought is led into an attempt to define the significance of the games. The contests match heroes with heroes, and approximate the epic battles where man fought god on plains of dubious battle. Perhaps, too, the Hesiodic battle of god and Titan suggests the image of the games. The contest at Olympia where Alcimidas lost, but almost won, completes the cycle begun by the original judgment in which man was found weaker than his brother, god. That contest and the present one are the poet's concern; and in this ode, the poet emerges from the opening theme and forms at the end of the poem the bridge back to the ornamentation of the concluding games. The center of the poem belongs to the athletes —all of them. Symmetry is achieved in this section by the summary list of Praxidamas' victories (Olympia, Isthmia, Nemea) and the balanced but much more extended praise of Callias, no doubt some more distant kinsman of Alcimidas: a Pythian victory replaces the Olympic, and the Isthmian and Nemean games are brilliantly ornamented. This cycle enshrines again, in the poem's center, the poet, who, in his own way, is an athlete too, but more important, is spoken of as the guardian of the past and present greatness of his patrons:

. . . . Guide straight this arrow from my bow, O Muse,
This high wind
Of poetry and fame: . . .
In fields where the Pierides plough,
What abundance these princes promise! Prized deeds for the
     poet
To hymn!

The patrons perform in the contests; the poet tends Mother Earth, genetrix of gods and men.

NEMEA VI: For Alcimidas of Aegina: Victory in Wrestling, Boys' Division

EN ΑΝΔΡΩΝ

STROPHE

One,
Men and gods —one race. From a single mother
The life we both breathe. But sundered when our every
    strength
Is brought to judgment: for us nothing and all is theirs:
    bronze
Estates secure forever
Abides their firmament. Nonetheless, the poet's mind some
    way,
The athlete's body —these approximate divinity,
Although in light of day nor night we cannot know
What die was cast,
What goal was traced toward which we run.

ANTISTROPHE

Witness:
Here is now Alcimidas: behold his stock

Is as the fields in tillage bearing harvest where lean years
Follow fat: the plains' gift sometimes is abundance,
Life for us a twelvemonth;
Sometimes fallow they rest and hoard their energy. See:
He is come from lovely Nemea, from the games, where
This boy contested, tracking down what Zeus ordains —
Endowment now made
Manifest: there in the arena he was a huntsman

EPODE

Treading step by step in the footprints of his family,
Of his father's father, Praxidamas,
That Olympic victor who had first brought Aeacos' tribe
A branch from the olives of the Alpheos
(And more: five times at the Isthmos crowned;
At Nemea thrice) —he ended the obscurity
Of Saocleides, eldest
Of the sons of Hagesimachos.

STROPHE

Three
In all, victors each come to the pinnacle
Of excellence —and each tasted the glory of Contest. As god
Willed, so no other house had boxing shown
Forth to be steward
Of more wreaths, here even in this treasury of all of Greece.
A high claim: but I expect to hit the target
Square. Guide straight this arrow from my bow, O Muse,
This high wind
Of poetry and fame: for men pass on,

ANTISTROPHE

But the singer
And the song escort from oblivion the beauty that was theirs.
Of such these sons of Bassos have known no dearth —a line
Ancient in nobility: a ship they come with cargo of encomia;
In fields where the Pierides plough,

Nemea VI

What abundance these princes promise! Prized deeds for the
    poet
To hymn! Yes: at Pytho the Holy, his hands
Bound in rawhide, remember, he, too, was a man
Of this blood: Callias
In triumph, who delighted the twin branch

EPODE

Of Leto (all of gold is her hair); there by Castalia
At sunset he blazed in the grace
Of ovation. And the bridge through the tireless sea —there
    where a bull
Is slaughtered at biennial games—
Honored this prince in the Sanctuary of Poseidon;
And the Lion-plant roofed him victor in the dense
Shadow of Phlious'
Primeval mountains.

STROPHE

Broad
Avenues from everywhere here converge: the eloquent
Escort this island to its praise. How not, when these the sons
Of Aeacos are our commission, our theme, our roster of
    grandeur
And excellence? Winged is their name:
Far, so far it flies, above the land, across
The sea. The distance even to Ethiopia: it hovered
In flight, swooped down, for Memnon had no journey home.
    "Achilles!"—
The name fell
A plague to earth: "He stepped from his chariot;

ANTISTROPHE

And our shining
Dawn's son he stripped, slain in the rage
Of his sword's edge." That was the royal road those
Who went before me found: I myself now follow it

77

And care for it my melody.
And yet it is the nearest wave, swirling at the ship's rudder —
As they say— that ever sets a maelstrom in our desire.
So, willingly, I track down this double burden for my back;
I step forth,
A herald to clarion this five and twentieth

EPODE

Proclamation, victory in the Games, whose epithets are
    sacred.
Alcimidas, you approached the mark
Of your famous family: You were two at Cronian's sanctuary,
    you
And Polytimidas; luck ill-matched you
With opponents and kept you from the Flowers of Olympia.
But to the dolphin in its swiftness through the sea I would
    liken
Melesias, the reinsman
Of your limbs and strength.

OLYMPIA VI: The Two Worlds of Pindar: "The Horses' Heads Were Toward Eternity"

For few poets is the journey to the essential structures of reality so painless as it was for Pindar. The humble mules, transformed by their victory at Olympia, know the way; the poet need only follow where they lead. Phintis the charioteer yokes up his team and the poet stages a pilgrimage which begins in the present and passes out through the gates of the city to end many generations earlier at Pitana, a city which, incarnate, is parent of our hero's greatness.

Truth is what the poetized phrase has codified; it is a nation's heritage, and the present can rank amongst the truths of reality only when it, too, is made to match the patterns of the past. The poet must have double sight. He sees, for example, the great priest-prophet Amphiaraos, who fought in the expedition of the Seven against Thebes. His life is history, caught eternally in the poetry which mnemonically holds the treasures of the past. The poet superimposes this pattern upon the present and, by so doing, measures the greatness of the victor, Hagesias. The eulogy that a past poet had coined for Amphiaraos can be applied unchanged to Hagesias, for he too is both a soldier and a priest. Once applied, the poetized item of knowledge itself passes into the treasure-house. The Muses now safeguard for the future Pindar's verdict, his own equation of the past and present.

Phintis' journey, then, is more than a brilliant poetic conceit. The mere act of journeying in this ode makes him the major statement in a series of variations, a pilgrimage to discover the hero's greatness. Aepytos travels to Pytho to inquire about the parentage of the illegitimate child his ward Evadne is to bear; he learns that Apollo himself was its sire and that the child will be prophetically inspired. And the child that is born, Iamos, the founder of Hagesias' line, is himself ordered, like Phintis, to journey:

Arise, O son: my Word leads to a land cosmopolite.

He is given his identity, a people who will esteem him, and the gift of prophecy at Zeus' altar at Olympia. Pindar, then, is impresario. Phintis follows the directions of his *metteur en scène* and the present so structured easily fits the significant action of the past.

Just as poet and athlete complement each other in the attempt to "approximate divinity," Phintis' journey is balanced in this ode by the journey of Aeneas, the chorus-leader, who will take the poem to Syracuse, Hagesias' second home at the court of the tyrant Hieron.

. . . . this cortège of Hagesias' revelry,
Which winds its way from Stymphalos' walls homewards
    from home,
Metropolis in Arcady's lush pasturage. How good
In the night sea-tempest from scudding
Ship to plummet down a double anchorage!

The poem has thus progressed from the splendor of its opening metaphor —the comparison of the ode to a mansion grand enough to house the victor's fame— to the actual palace on Quail-Island, Ortygia. The poem has realized the "façade from far effulgent," which now, no longer in Stymphalos, shines from Syracuse across the ocean, to welcome the hero and his cortège home. Phintis had journeyed from the poet's city back into myth; from the poem emerges a true journey, but one that perhaps merely completes the first, and develops poetically from the two treasure-houses which, in the myth, Iamos had found at the end of his journey.

The poet, then, manipulates present reality to form an analogue of the past. The present, when thus seen, can sound with the resonance of its full meaning, for it is this harmonious correspondence which marks for Pindar the truth of what he says. It is this very process that must occur as the poet writes his poem. A thought, when it first hovers in his mind, is somewhat formless; it does not fit the demands of his meter or perhaps even the formulae of his own clichés. At the moment of its coincidence with the pre-established form, however, it seems to have been inevitable; the vision is brought into a sudden focus, and the phrase, which is now rhythmic, is heard against the instruments that will accompany it:

> The thought upon my tongue is whetstone-honed to resonance
> And creeps upon me —O may it come!— with the liquid
> Breath of flutes.

That is to say, the thought has been poetized and has therefore become an item of knowledge.

But to live in the tradition, the poem must have its performance. What has been encoded must be deciphered. Aeneas is his scytala,* the proof that the poet's message is

* Pindar is here referring to the Spartan method of sending coded messages. The message was written on a strip of leather which had been wound spirally around a stick of a particular diameter. Since the line of writing extended along the length of the stick and repeatedly crossed the breaks in the wound thong, the message when unwound would be unreadable until wrapped again around another stick of the same diameter. The scytala was the stick used for the code system. One piece of it remained with the sender, the other with the recipient; and the message itself was proved authentic if it was intelligible when wrapped around the recipient's scytala.

authentic. Aeneas' presence in Syracuse will both sign the poem as Pindar's and truthfully interpret the poem's meaning. In this role of intermediary, Aeneas again corresponds to Phintis, who in his performance at Olympia showed forth not his own athletic brilliance but the grandeur and divinity that emanate from Hagesias.

———————

The poet's thought in this ode repeatedly returns to the significance of the poetizing process. We have seen that Amphiaraos, reduced to a poetic formula, was used as a canon by which to judge Hagesias. The Theban prophet's position in the ode is wreathed by the poet's meditation upon the curious phenomenon of coincidence of past and present. (It is this cyclic structure which Professor Norwood at this point has misinterpreted when he writes of two statements relative to Amphiaraos. There is only one statement; the poet says that the phrase has been already coined, states the phrase, and then again says that he will testify that Amphiaraos' eulogy fits Hagesias.) This meditation returns toward the end of the ode when the poet forms his own succinct phrase, his own poetic conceit, that links him to his victor's city, Stymphalos. For the Theban poet is genealogically linked to the hero: he is a child of the nymph-city Thebe, whose mother was Metope of Stymphalos. The phrase is introduced by his excited statement that his thought has suddenly fit the pattern, and it is concluded by a return to a meditation on the nature of poetry, which acts as a transition to the directions given to Aeneas.

The victor's name is similarly embedded in meditation on the function of poetry. The cliché that excellence incites jealousy develops quite naturally from the magnificent palace the poet builds:

—if but the beauty
Of our song incite no neighbor's jealousy . . . .
Take heed: it is this sandal fits your saintly foot, O son

Of Sostratos! And yet . . . an excellence with nothing
Ventured gains no honor, be you statesman or sail
The hollow ships; for perfection, run the risk and many will
    remember.

Remembering is, of course, accomplished once the victor's
excellence has been poetized. The statement therefore not
only acts as transition to the section relative to Amphiaraos,
but also recurs in the instructions to Aeneas. Perhaps the
praise of Hieron is meant to allay that neighbor's jealousy:

I instructed you remember Syracuse and its island of Ortygia,
    where sceptered
Hieron holds holy sway.

The jealousy-cliché is restated when the poet again mentions
the victor's name:

                             Prize
Excellence and you walk a road conspicuous where all
Things test your worth; the others envy, poised with the
    brand
Of Censure, if once you round the twelfth lap
First and grace divine rains
Down renown and beauty.

That the victor comes from Stymphalos is at the same time
transition to the Thebe-conceit and the close for the jealousy-
cliché: Hermes, who holds the people of Stymphalos in
special esteem, will guard and insure the continuance of
Hagesias' good fortune:

                    Why then, he, O son
Of Sostratos, and the thunder-heavy father are regents of
    your luck!

It was originally the fear, or rather the poetically assumed fear, that had led Pindar modestly to reapply the
Amphiaraos phrase; life is uncertain and excessive praise is

ruined if an adverse critic notes its exaggeration. But the poet as he now again returns to Hagesias is not satisfied with his previous modesty. Hagesias is preternaturally fortunate in his close association with Hermes: perhaps the victor this time is less subject to vicissitude; perhaps greater praise might be hazarded. Pindar, too, has reason to see good omen for his endeavor. His connections with Stymphalos incite him to think that the poem might attain greater heights. The poem, however, or the actual phrase of eulogy, is never stated: the ode in its mythological narrative has turned toward the future and has carried with it the poet's eulogy, which is converted into the directions to Aeneas—the performance of the ode which has not yet happened. The neighbor who might be jealous now owns the house and welcomes to it his friend, together with the procession for the song that must yet be sung. The praise of Hagesias comports the future's limitless possibilities.

The interrelated themes of jealousy, Hagesias, the poetized phrase, Amphiaraos (or, in the second treatment, Thebe), form a major frame for the myth proper. It will be seen from the diagram that the directions to Phintis function as the immediate transition to the myth; the balancing address to Aeneas does not occur at the end of the myth but develops from the meditation on the poetized phrase, and is again used to introduce a journey, the trip to the second house of Hagesias. It may be that the motif has been displaced from its position in the ring-structure in order that it might fulfill its dual function of simple transition and, together with the two other journeys, major reflection of the poem's meaning. It is, after all, in the nature of a journey to move forward, even though the goal of the journey may be the past.

Outward from the ode's antrum of myth —Pitana and Poseidon, Evadne and Apollo, Aepytos, Iamos— flame royalty and sunburst, the gold and purple sifting through the poem, but concentrated in the mythic core, the treasure-house. Ring-composition, epinician clichés, motif variations, whereby both the *fond* and the *forme* are structured and maintained in cohesion, are permeated by that pervasive coloration of "Olympia VI" which has delighted even the dustiest academicians. Color persuades, clarifies, and makes coherent. Surely it is the double nature of Hagesias —the Olympic victor simultaneously steward of Zeus at Pisa and founding father of Syracuse— or, rather, the double nature of the whole line of Iamids, that provokes Pindar to wash his ode in gold and purple.

Gold gleam the pillars of the house, the mansion, the poem, the "palatial hymn," the dazzling façade across the water, the Turner-like effulgence from which the poem journeys and to which it returns; Amphiaraos' horses shine in the crimson flames of pyres; Pitana sleeps with wine-dark Poseidon and her child's hair is a sheen of black and violet; Evadne is possessed by the god of the Sun; Aepytos travels to the Sun's shrine at Pytho while Evadne's pitcher glows in the blue thicket beside her crocus-crimson sash; serpents with metallic eyes guard Iamos:

> hidden in rushes, in a briery tangle inaccessible,
> He lay, his tender body drenched
> In the sunburst dew of violets
> All topazine and purpurean.

Iamos' youth grows to ripeness and is crowned in gold; he wades in the blue water and invokes the purple of Poseidon, the gold of Apollo; the word of gold resounds in the purple night; gold treads the rock of Zeus where future treasures shine; Hieron celebrates Demeter, whose feet are dyed in the colors of harvest, and Kore, brought back from shadow by the horses' light. Anchors plunge through the sea. In a golden haze Hagesias' cortège moves over the water, back to the mansion, the portico, the golden pillars. Amphitrite spins the sea to gold.

Theme A (1-4)   The House of Eulogy
Theme B (4-12)   envy cliché
                         son of Sostratos —Hagesias
                     envy cliché
Theme C (12-21)   poetized phrase: the past phrase reapplied
                         Amphiaraos (Theban reference)
                     poetized phrase
Theme D: Prelude to E (22-28)   Address to Phintis: athletic
                                     performance and journey to
                                     the past
Theme E (29-72)   Purpose: to tell the origin of the Iamids
                         The central myth, including Apollo's
                         directions (theme D) for Iamos' jour-
                         ney toward the future: the prophet's
                         performance
                     Purpose achieved
Theme B (72-81)   envy cliché
                         Hagesias —son of Sostratos
                     envy cliché: the victor's Arcadian parent-
                         age is an omen of success indicating that
                         perhaps he is less subject to vicissitude.
Theme C (82-87)   poetized phrase: the new eulogy
                         Metope-Thebe (Theban reference)
                     poetized phrase: not the actual eulogy, but
                         the omen that what the poet will say will
                         be successful.
Theme D: Prelude to A (87-91)   Address to Aeneas: poetic
                                     performance and journey
                                     toward the future poem (in-
                                     cluding the Hera Parthenia
                                     prelude which will rein-
                                     state the two favorable Ar-
                                     cadian omens).
Theme A (92-105)   The Double House. Envy escaped, for the
                         victor's house of eulogy is his neighbor's.

OLYMPIA VI: For Hagesias of Syracuse: Victory With Mule-Team

Sung at Stymphalos; Again at Syracuse

ΧΡΤΣΕΑΣ ΤΠΟΣΤΑΣΑΝΤΕΣ ΕΤΤΕΙΧΕΙ ΠΡΟΘΤΡΩΙ ΘΑΛΑΜΟΤ

STROPHE

They golden stand beneath the solid mansion's portico —
Pillars that I place to build this hall,
This cynosure: for the work begins, and we must fashion
Its façade from far effulgent. Yes, but suppose our victor is
      Olympic,
Trustee at the mantic shrine of Zeus in Pisa,
A founding father of the glory that is Syracuse:
What palatial hymn
Could he not enter? —if but the beauty
Of our song incite no neighbor's jealousy . . . .

ANTISTROPHE

Take heed: it is this sandal fits your saintly foot, O son
Of Sostratos! And yet . . . an excellence with nothing
Ventured gains no honor, be you statesman or sail
The hollow ships; for perfection, run the risk and many will
      remember.

87

Hagesias, your eulogy has been already coined: Adrastos
Aptly voiced it, apropos of Oecles'
Prophetic son, Amphiaraos
(Down had borne the Earth on him,
Had seized him and his horses sleek and shining):

EPODE

Seven they were, pyres consuming corpses, and then Talaos'
    son
Spoke at Thebes: "Our eye were not more dear
Than he, my army's seer —
Great prophet no less good in combat." How apposite
A phrase to catch this Syracusan master of our revels —
I crave no quarrel nor thrive in rivalry—:
I by my oath here bear him witness
Clearly; and Muses —the voice of honey— safe-guard my
    verdict.

STROPHE

Up, then Phintis, O harness me your mules' sheer strength!
For theirs is the swiftness —our carriage once come
To the high road— leads us back to birth
Of heroes. Yes, this team, beyond all others, knows what way
To guide our journey's course, for wreaths at Olympia
Have decked them. Throw wide the gates
Of song before them! Pitana
Is our goal, she by the Eurotas-ford: ours
To seize this day the fitting moment.

ANTISTROPHE

Hear then how she, they say, slept with Poseidon Cronios
And bore a child, the violet-haired Evadne.
She had hidden her maternity —virgin labor— beneath
Her robes, and then, her months accomplished, sent servants
    with orders
To entrust to great Eilatides her infant to be raised.
(His subjects were Arcadians —his court at Phaesana;

But his realm extended to the Alpheos.)
She grew up there, and Apollo's hand
Awoke her first delight in Aphrodite —

EPODE

Not unnoticed: for Aepytos suspected the embryo of god
She'd cached away. He went to Pytho —cold reason
Repressing rage unspeakable—
To seek an answer of the priestess: how endure this suffering,
     this insult?
The girl meanwhile was setting her crocus-crimson sash
Aside, and her ewer of silver; and in the blueness
Of a thicket bore her prophetic son.
(The gold-haired god had stationed in attendance Eleithyia
     and the Moerae.)

STROPHE

He came from her womb, from love's labor —her child,
     Iamos,
Eased into day's light. She was vexed,
Left him on the ground; but behold: two steel-eyed —
For the gods had planned it that he so be raised— serpents
     (but their venom was harmless,
Like honey of the stinging bees) to nourish him. And the
     king . . . ?
Back home from his ride to rocky Pytho,
He questioned all the servants of his household:
Where was that son Evadne bore?
For Phoebos, he said, had been its sire —

ANTISTROPHE

"A child, the future prophet to mankind, beyond all others
Preeminent. And his line shall never perish."
Such his revelation. But —"I never heard of him,"
They swore; "Never saw him." And the infant, five days old!
     No:
For hidden in rushes, in a briery tangle inaccessible,

He lay, his tender body drenched
In the sunburst dew of violets
All topazine and purpurean. Whence his mother
Called him Iamos, which means "Porphyry

EPODE

The Violet-child," a name immortal. When grown to harvest
    pleasures
That golden-crown young manhood, in Alpheos midstream
    he waded,
Invoked from lordly realms
His grandfather Poseidon and the bowman who sentries
    Delos, that god
Built. He begged esteem, a people —his coronal.
It was night; the air clear: distinct,
The paternal voice resounded, sought him:
"Arise, O son: my Word leads to a land cosmopolite."

STROPHE

And they came to the rock of lofty Cronion —where the sun
    walks.
There a treasure-house of prophecy doubly
He endowed: "The first you hear already, this voice
That knows no lie; and later when the Stalwart comes,
    Heracles the adroit,
That august branch of the Alcaeid tree, when he founds
His father's holiday and institutes the Great
Games, where the crowds throng:
Then at Zeus's most high altar
I command you to establish a shrine oracular" —

ANTISTROPHE

A day whenceforth all Greece has glorified the clan of Iamids.
Success followed in attendance. Prize
Excellence and you walk a road conspicuous where all
Things test your worth; the others envy, poised with the
    brand

Olympia VI

Of Censure, if once you round the twelfth lap
First and grace divine rains
Down renown and beauty.
Is it not true your mother's people,
Hagesias, dwelling in the foothills of Cyllene,

Have offered many a gift to Hermes, the herald of the gods,
Always in piety, with rural simplicity? (His
Are the Games, he presides at Contests;
Noble Arcadia is his.) Why then, he, O son
Of Sostratos, and the thunder-heavy father are regents of
  your luck!
The thought upon my tongue is whetstone-honed to
  resonance
And creeps upon me —O may it come!— with the liquid
Breath of flutes: My mother's mother flowered in Stymphalos,

Metope: her child was Thebe, Equestrienne, whose land's
  rivers
I shall drink in love, weaving for warriors
Daedal song. Rouse the chorus now,
Aeneas, first to hymn with music's surge Hera Parthenia:
Then shall we know if truly we escape reproach —
That ancient insult of "Boeotian swine!"
For you are my forthright messenger;
My chevelurèd Muses' code you verify —
Commingling krater of psalmody's sweet wines.

I instructed you remember Syracuse and its island of Ortygia,
  where sceptered
Hieron holds holy sway:
His way is justness. He celebrates his suzerain, Demeter
(Who treads the russet harvest); the Daughter's festival
  (white stallions brought

91

Her back); and Zeus of Aetna's power. Dulcet
Voice of lyres, the dance know him.
May Time's encroachment leave
Prosperity unroiled! May he welcome there
In friendship this cortège of Hagesias' revelry,

EPODE

Which winds its way from Stymphalos' walls homewards
    from home,
Metropolis in Arcady's lush pasturage. How good
In the night sea-tempest from scudding
Ship to plummet down a double anchorage! O god
Benign, their theme in glory grant these cities!
Lord Oceans'-King, guide this crossing
Free from shipwreck! —thou mate of Amphitrite,
Who spins the sea to gold. Let swell this poem to flowerage!

Isthmia VIII: An Athlete's Requiem

Achilles was born to die. All of the hero's epic brilliance is here in Pindar's ode but a parenthesis, a summary catalog that bridges the period from birth to death. Themis had spoken in the parliament of gods; she had preserved the divine hierarchy and thwarted the unborn Achilles' heredity. If his mother, Thetis, had united with a fellow-deity, the child would have been divine and greater than his father. Destiny, however, was compromised, and the great Achilles limps through life with one mortal parent. The young hero's career is but a pale reflection of the surpassing power that would have been his.

It is upon this paradigm of youth in death that Pindar builds his memorial poem for the boxer, Nicocles, whose war at Troy was fought against the Persian invaders. War and the national athletic contests were the opportunities a Greek had to achieve epiphany. When Achilles died, the Muses themselves sang his requiem; Pindar, who is related to the Aeginetan nobility through the sister-nymphs Thebe and Aegina, is particularly inspired to follow the goddesses' precedent.

But grief is a poor guest at celebration. Pindar assumes

for himself the family's sorrow, and with exquisite balance tempers it with the festivity proper to the young Cleandros' victory. The cousin's triumph and the jubilation of his comrades redeem in part past loss. The poem not only ransoms Cleandros from the fatigue of his own athletic endeavor, but also represents the release that song brings to sorrow. We must cease from pointless sufferings:

> for what
> There is at hand demands the more
> Attention always. Impending Time
> Insidious twists our life's channel, but Freedom heals us
> Even that. Cherish good expectations.

The transition is one which Pindar uses elsewhere to justify his turning from a past hero to the present victor. What has happened has happened, and yet in some way we have the freedom to cure or change what has been destined. This is the lesson that Themis teaches: the destined fall of Zeus is avoided by a diplomatic marriage. The poet's control of language can redeem man's mortal state. The fragility of human glory, that very quality of which Achilles is the epitome, achieves in poetry its measure of immortality. It is an action in which the hero and poet collaborate. After the sorrow of Greece's intolerable agony; after the private griefs collectively made public in the symbol of Greece's rock of Tantalos; after the Persian threat had passed (despite the modern critics, the political reference extends perhaps not beyond this line: the grief is for funeral, not for the treacherous role Thebes played in siding with the Mede, nor for the punishment Greece exacted from the Theban nobles; Nicocles' memorial structurally balances the earlier theme of grief, which is itself framed at the beginning and end of the ode by the theme of Cleandros' youth); Cleandros and his poet appear as saviors:

> O, may we not fall all orphaned of our crowns.

Cleandros belongs to youth; his eulogy is sung by young men. Nicocles belongs to the dead. The poet's song redeems the victor; the victory compensates for death, and the dead have liberated Greece. The same virtuosity or excellence is made to seem in Achilles' life a succession of saving acts, for, despite his character better known to us from the *Iliad*, he here bridges the seas homeward for the Atrides and sets Helen free, thus blazoning in epiphany his stock, Aegina. The mention of Aegina returns us to the conceit with which Pindar had introduced the myth, the passage in which the poet presents his credentials for this ode:

> A man was raised in Thebes of the Seven Gates
> Destined to proffer to Aegina a quintessential grace.

The reverberations are complex. By repeating the acts of Achilles, Pindar adds his voice to that of the Ancients. Achilles, no less than Cleandros, depends on Pindar. The Muses of Helicon who sang the epic hero's requiem are Pindar's precedent, as he here turns the funeral of Nicocles to public celebration.

The tonality of liberation and freedom has in fact filigreed the ode's main structure. The words "release," "freedom," "ransom," "good expectation," "halt," "cease," "deliverance," color the major themes. Even Thetis, whose marriage forms the topic for the parliament of gods and is thus the central section of the extended Aegina-ornamentation, is said at the moment of her union with Peleus to untie the bridle of her virginity. Her mortal marriage frees the gods from the threat of destiny just as, paradoxically, the poet frees the mortal hero from his destined mortality.

It is this graceful ornament which gives the poem its peculiar poignancy; for the poem is not one of Pindar's most brilliant, and yet the strong intimation it expresses that youth and its promise for the future may redeem our mutilated lives moves us, perhaps with less confidence than it did Pindar, to hope that all is not mere bravado before the void.

What is destined was for a Greek perhaps destined only if one blithely accepted the terms as stated. As Themis showed, and Pindar too, a slight change, a compromise, a graceful balance, can lead to mastery over what had seemed ordained. Funeral can be our festival.

Isthmia VIII: For Cleandros of Aegina:
Victory in the Boys' Pancration:
Dedicated to Nicocles in Memoriam

ΚΛΕΑΝΔΡΩΙ ΤΙΣ ΑΛΙΚΙΑΙ ΤΕ ΛΥΤΡΟΝ

STROPHE

For Cleandros and youth time: you young men go
With glory, free him from fatigue!
Stand you, someone, in the stately courtyard
Of Telesarchos, his father: rouse
Festivities —Isthmian victory-ransom and Nemea's,
For he has found his strength in Contest. Yes, I too, though
    grieved
At heart, am asked to summon him the golden
Muse. After great our sorrows, now deliverance!
O, may we not fall all orphaned of our crowns,
Nor nurse our mournings! I cease from pointless sufferings,
And public shall be our celebration, even after anguish:
Look! the rock of Tantalos
Above our heads someone —a god— has turned aside,

STROPHE

Has ended Greece's agony intolerable.
Enough! As panic passed

It called a halt to my anxiety: for what
There is at hand demands the more
Attention always. Impending Time
Insidious twists our life's channel, but Freedom heals us
Even that. Cherish good expectations:
A man was raised in Thebes of the Seven Gates
Destined to proffer to Aegina a quintessential grace.
Why? Half-sisters were sired of Asopos, his youngest
Two, and both pleased Zeus the King,
Who settled one as sovereign
Of Charioteers in a city where Dirce's spring flows beautiful;

STROPHE

And you to this island wineland he brought,
Aegina: of your love the saintlike
Aeacos was born; and his father, who hefts
The thunder, cherished him exceeding
And even of gods made him the judge.
Of immortal peerage were his sons and their sons squires to
    Ares:
Vassalage par excellence in the clangor of bronze
And lamentation. Yet wisdom held their wits in balance.
These qualities the parliament of gods remembered, when
    Zeus
Contended with the splendor of Poseidon, each courting
Thetis for her beauty, each wanting her his own;
But passion had possessed them
In vain: divinities' immortal sentence forbade love's

STROPHE

Consummation, lent ear to oracles. She spoke
In council —wise Themis:
"Destiny," she said. The sea-goddess would bear
A king for son stronger
Than his father, one whose hand would hurl
A greater bolt than thunder, than trident's ravage —should
    she

98

Conceive by Zeus or Zeus's brothers.
"Prevent it! Let her sleep in mortal bed and look
Upon a son dead in battle, whose hands
Were strong as Ares', whose feet outflashed the lightning.
You ask my verdict. Give her Godspeed as wife
To Peleus, Aeacos' son —
No man, they say, more pious has Iaolchos plain brought
    forth.

STROPHE

Quick! Go send word
To ageless Chiron's cave!
Let Nereus' daughter not hand us
Twice the ballots of our discord!
At the mid-month, in evenings of the full moon,
I see her love of Peleus untie the bridle of her virginity."
She spoke to princes of the blood, and they
With eyes immortal nodded in assent; nor did her words
Wither before their harvest. The commonweal, they say,
Was both the Kings' concern: Thetis was married.
To generations the mouths of poets made manifest the young
Achilles' excellence, who showered
Blood-black the vineyard plains of Mysia with gore of
    Telephos,

STROPHE

And homeward bridged the seas for Atrides;
Helen he freed, his spear
Severing Troy's Sinews (who thwarted him
In the field amid his marshalled
Crests of War, the Despoiler) —Memnon,
I mean, and Hector the Bold and their entourage of princes.
    They entered
The secret mansions of Persephone Achilles
Showed —champion of the Aeacids, who blazoned in
    epiphany

His stock, Aegina. Him not even dead did song
Desert, but by his pyre and by his tomb
The virgins of Helicon stood: in requiem flowed
Their consort of voices. By divine
Decree, greatness that died was granted the goddesses'
    psalmody —

STROPHE

Our precedent today: look! the Muses'
Chariot speeds to sound
Memorial to the boxer Nicocles. Honor him,
Who in the forest of the Isthmus
Earned his wreath of Dorian smallage,
For he, too, beat the contenders there with a welter
Of fists! His noble uncle's son
Is not unworthy of him: for Cleandros let
Someone young weave the grace of myrtle,
A Crown Pancration. (The Alcathoos Games
And the athletes at Epidauros had earlier claimed him
    victor.)
A prince might praise him: his years
Of youth he did not bury obscured, untouched by beauty.

Pythia VIII: On the Road to Delphi

Conditioned as we are today to suspect all non-rational experience as the product of a sick mind, we are startled by Pindar's mention of his own personal encounter with the spirit of the dead prophet, Alcmaeon. Professor Norwood has called attention to our contemporary uneasiness, noticing that critics persist in emasculating this experience by relegating it to the status of a mere dream-phenomenon. No dream is specifically indicated, and we must admit the possibility of waking miracles in ancient Greece. Pindar was, after all, on the road to Delphi, the oracular shrine where a woman's hysterical delusions were accepted as the god's revealed truth. A culture that would seek out and so elevate such madness must certainly differ greatly from our own. . . . Dream or not, for Pindar the encounter was real and is the significant proof of his devious argument in the poem he wrote in his old age for Aristomenes of Aegina.

> And myself, I second his rejoicing, falling
> Wreaths on Alcmaeon, asperging him with song:
> For he, my neighbor, guardian of my riches,
> Met me as I traveled to the fabled Navel of the Earth;
> And practiced his inherited prophetic art.

We are of course tempted to inquire about the content of Alcmaeon's prophecy. This is not immediately relevant. Alcmaeon is mentioned as someone whom Pindar has trusted (he is indeed the poet's banker: the temples of antiquity were moderately safe depositories for movable wealth) and who has now vouchsafed his devotee an epiphany. That he prophesies is for Pindar evidence that the son, Alcmaeon, has inherited his father Amphiaraos' oracular art. It is this fact which closes the mythic section that had begun with the promise that something Amphiaraos had said was particularly apposite to the victor's situation. Amphiaraos, the prophet-warrior who saw *troppo davante,* who in the first expedition to Thebes was swallowed by the earth, is a spectator when the sons of the Seven reverse their fathers' defeat. The line of heroes has heroes for progeny. "Behold the fathers' noble/Temperament innative in their sons."

In its most narrow reference, Amphiaraos' comment applies to Aristomenes, who has followed in the footsteps of his maternal uncles, Theognetos and Cleitomachos. He is, of course, only "this latest debt to beauty"; for the poet, in a magnificent break-off formula, has turned his attention from the full roster of Aeginetan heroes to the present, "this that races by." But success, like Christian grace, retains an element of the unpredictable. It is in this direction that the Amphiaraos-motto receives its narrative ornamentation: Adrastos, who alone of the Captains survived the first defeat, now sees his son the only casualty of the second expedition.

The significance of this unpredictability is difficult, if not dangerous, for Pindar to express: it requires a special prayer for Apollo's aid in choosing the right words for each of the rapidly shifting sections that follow:

> O King, I pray it please you look
> Somewhat in harmony on each
> And every by-way of the poem I modulate.

The poet's commission is just ("Justice attends our revel's melody") but this alone will not insure the victor's continu-

ing success. In an earlier poem the poet had attempted to
explain the phenomenon of a noble family's vicissitudes by
the metaphor of the fields which sometimes lie fallow, only
thus to regain their strength. Pindar's view is darker now
and more brilliant, a triumphant pessimism. Luck, the unpredictable dispensation of grace, is master of man's condition. If anyone thinks Xenarkes' family effortlessly fortunate
simply because they are clever businessmen, it is a sad mistake:

> .... such things lie not in man's control —god is their
>   provenience,
> Who tosses high, then pins one in his grip.

A Greek's action is overdetermined. His own private awareness of free will makes it impossible to believe in a source
of motivation outside himself. He accepts responsibility for
his actions; there would be no glory in heroism if the hero
did not fight to earn what he wins. And yet actions often end
where they were not intended, or one does what one does
not mean. Such actions are disavowed; they cannot be the
doer's, or if they are, someone else has made him do them.
Indeed, a prophet could not prophesy, were there no plan
to a man's actions, although this plan may be only the prophet's foreknowledge that an individual will freely choose a
certain course of action. If in this poem Pindar places the
greater emphasis on determination beyond man's control, it
is only to make the significance of his victory the more brilliant. It is true that inherited nobility will predispose one to
a position of leadership, but if an individual through his own
effort brings to realization his inheritance, he must acknowl-
edge that success was achieved under the sign of god, that
god, as it were, has renewed his pact with the hero.

   This meditation forms the poet's introduction to the victory-catalog, balancing his earlier choice to turn from past
to present triumph. Its significance for the victor is to caution humility. What god gives, he can take away: "Step

softly to the ring." The ensuing list climaxes with the Pythian victory, already mentioned twice before in this poem; but the triumph is stated this time first in a minor tonality, for the focus is placed on those who had no luck, the four who "down back streets . . . cower, on tenter-hooks from the sting of shame." This is what Aristomenes might have been, had god so willed. He, however, stands in the sunburst; he soars on high, the flight that Pindar had promised in the earlier break-off formula:

> But the one who wins just now
> His splendor soars —for hope is realized—
> In grandest affluence
> On the wings of prowess, to more
> Than wealth aspiring.

It is as though the younger Pindar had seen only the obverse: his treatment of the vicissitude theme had been merely lip-service to one of the clichés of his poetry, a kind of insurance protecting his patron's magnificence. For the first time, we feel with him our true fragility. God is the juggler, wrestler, perhaps the referee:

> In a moment man is magnified
> To ecstasy; a moment, and he earthward falls:
> A judgment's turn has shattered joy.
> O mutability of man! What is he? What is he not? A shadow's
> Dream. . . . But when the sunburst Zeus gift comes, a lambent aureole
> Rests on men and life is balm.

The concluding prayer to Aegina returns us to the invocation to Hesychia or the quietude of Civic Concord, and reminds us of the greater burden Pindar makes the victory of Aristomenes bear. Hesychia is no cult-goddess (although she is here so honored), but a conscious personification. She is a factionless agreement amongst the city's ruling class, the unified policy that produces peace at home and a strong front to face the world. A Greek god, however, controls not only his gift but the absence of that gift. Apollo, for example, who sends the plague, is the same deity whom doctors honor. Thus the man who offends Quietude learns, like the giants Typho and Porphyrion, the goddess' double nature. In her service both Zeus and Apollo acted when they destroyed the offenders and restored Concord to the heavenly hierarchy. By a simple parallelism, it was also in her service that Apollo honored Aristomenes: his victory is the ex-voto dedicated to the goddess. The political stability of Aegina must therefore have been responsible for his Pythic success. Since she is but a personification, since men have it in their power to govern their city in harmony, it would appear that the deities Zeus and Apollo do not act at random but serve a cosmic principle which does not entirely elude man's control. Even if man is the plaything of the gods, the game they must both play has moral determinants.

Aegina emerges as the particularization of the generic personification of Hesychia; they are linked by the similarity of epithets: Aegina who is named "this Justice citadel" recalls Hesychia, "the Cities' greatness . . . daughter of Justice," perhaps the same Justice which Pindar claims attends his revelry. In this complex interdependence of man, god, and ethical personification, it is difficult to know whether the great city has produced great men or whether the men have produced the city. They are in any case concomitant, and the initial cause was perhaps just irrational luck:

> A lucky throw not far
> From Grace this island.

Past glory is followed by the present instance, which, as we have seen, proves that heroism is an inherited trait.

It should be obvious that the meditation revolves, that it contains matter for an optimistic, as well as for the most somber, view of man's condition. What indeed is man? His mutable nature reflects the same dual manifestation of unity that was seen in Hesychia. He is both saint and nothing; he is the victor or, by a judgment's turn, the defeated; Aegina, the island whose glory was perfect *in principio,* can witness her own eclipse, for this had happened as Athens rose to power. But can so much glory perish? As Alcmaeon shows, ability is handed from father to son. Yet the prayer to Apollo cautions that even the fortunes of a great and noble family require the god's continued beneficence. We therefore earn what we are, inherit what we are, and receive what we are from god.

The conclusion can be nothing but a humble prayer. Aegina, the mother of heroes, will lead her city forward under the aegis of Hesychia in the company of her consort, Zeus, and her great men. The previously broken-off roster of Aeginetan heroes is now stated simply, for it is in them that the poet takes confidence for the future. It was they who signaled the greatness of the city and its government; such men will have descendants, like Aristomenes, who will be their heirs to greatness. The past phenomenon must, it is the poet's hope, repeat itself. The experience with Alcmaeon had provided the poet with the essential proof of inheritance, the basis for Pindar's cautious optimism that man will escape the apparent irrationality of god's treatment of him. Hesychia, the city's internal liberty, is something within man's control; and she acts, as it were, to stabilize vicissitude. The poem is a profound attempt to foist on heaven a humanly evolved ethical principle. The old gods seem to maintain their fickle independence —Pindar is no iconoclast— yet, within the terms of the traditional, the new thought strives to find expression. If there are confusions in the argument, they are no less startling than those of Aeschylus in his *Oresteia* some twelve years earlier, and they stem from the same cause: the use of the poetic-narrative language, which of necessity retains the past modes of thought, to essay the matter of philosophy.

Pythia VIII: For Aristomenes, Wrestler From Aegina

ΦΙΛΟΦΡΟΝ ΗΣΥΧΙΑ ΔΙΚΑΣ

STROPHE

Benefic Concord, the Cities'
Greatness, you, O daughter of Justice,
Who hold in sovereignty
The Keys of governments and wars,
Consecrate this victory, Aristomenes' Pythic homage.
For it is you who know unerringly what time
Fits gentleness in action or passivity.

ANTISTROPHE

But let a man drive home
To heart his rancorous choler: a savage
Adversary then
You counter him with force to bilge
The troublemakers' insolence —which fact Porphyrion
    learned
Too late in angering you: the profit's more prized
If the master give what is borne from his house.

EPODE

(Braggadocio's violence trips him up, if given time.)
Yes, not Cilician Typho with heads a hundredfold escaped;
Nor did that king of Giants: both blasted by thunderbolt
Or by Apollo's arrows, whose mind in kindness
Welcomed Xenarkes' son from Kirrha crowned
In Parnassus grass and Doric revelry.

STROPHE

A lucky throw not far
From Grace this island, this Justice citadel
Embracing excellence,
The fame of Aeacids, her glory
Perfect *in principio,* sung for highest heroes
Raised to bear home victory
In countless contests and the quick of battle.

ANTISTROPHE

Which qualities distinguish still
Her men today, but pressed for time
I cannot set
To lyre nor gentle voice
So full a roster: boredom grates. This
That races by: O soar this latest debt
To beauty, son, on wing of art!

EPODE

Deservedly: for you have tracked the footsteps of your
    mother's brothers; your wrestling
Has not shamed them: no, not Olympia's Theognetos nor the
    victory
Of sinew Cleitomachos won at Isthmus.
Exalter of your Meidylid clan, you bear
The motto Oecles' son devised: he saw
At seven-gated Thebes the dauphins stand

Pythia VIII

STROPHE

Their ground, when they had come from Argos,
Sons of the Seven, this second expedition.
He spoke as they battled:
"Behold the fathers' noble
Temperament innative in their sons. How marvelous!
My Alcmaeon first to brandish on spangled
Shield a serpent iridescent at Cadmos'

ANTISTROPHE

Gates; and he who suffered
The earlier debacle —the lord Adrastos—
Has now intelligence
Of more propitious augury —except
His private loss: he alone of the Danaean force
Will gather the bones of a son who died,
While his army, god willing, returns intact

EPODE

To the avenues of Abas, where victory choruses shall dance."
    Such
The pronouncement of Amphiaraos. And myself, I second
    his rejoicing, falling
Wreaths on Alcmaeon, asperging him with song:
For he, my neighbor, guardian of my riches,
Met me as I traveled to the fabled Navel of the Earth:
And practiced his inherited prophetic art.

STROPHE

You, the marksman Archer,
Whose famous temple in the Pythic hills
Sanctuaries all,
There you have bestowed the greatest
Of felicities; (earlier his home-town festival that honors you
Produced the pentathletic prize he took).
O King, I pray it please you look

ANTISTROPHE

Somewhat in harmony on each
And every by-way of the poem I modulate.
Justice attends
Our revel's melody; and I ask
The gods, Xenarkes, to continue smiling on your luck.
Yes, let someone painlessly succeed,
And the crowd will think him clever in the midst

EPODE

Of fools for having armed his life with scheming stratagems;
But such things lie not in man's control —god is their
    provenience,
Who tosses high, then pins one in his grip.
Step softly to the ring: at Megara you won,
And in the crook of the Marathon hills; and thrice you
    triumphed,
Aristomenes, in your city's games to Hera.

STROPHE

Four hulking bodies
To the dust you felled intent on their defeat,
Whose homecoming
Pytho judged no jubilee;
No lightsome laughter roused round them joy
In their mothers' welcome. Down back streets
They cower, on tenter-hooks from the sting of shame.

ANTISTROPHE

But the one who wins just now
His splendor soars —for hope is realized—
In grandest affluence
On the wings of prowess, to more
Than wealth aspiring. In a moment man is magnified
To ecstasy; a moment, and he earthward falls:
A judgment's turn has shattered joy.

Pythia VIII

O mutability of man! What is he? What is he not? A shadow's
Dream. . . . But when the sunburst Zeus gift comes, a
    lambent aureole
Rests on men and life is balm.
Aegina, beloved mother, in liberty
Escort this city: with Zeus, the lord Aeacos,
Peleus, good Telamon, and with Achilles.

OLYMPIA II: Deliverance From Time

Not all who die die. A few escape the vicissitude which, in the repeatedly broached meditation that ornaments this ode's central mythic section, emerges as more than this world's temporal changes of fortune, for it is seen to reach beyond our death in the Pythagorean-Orphic cycles of re-incarnation. Against the darker foil of suffering, perhaps, on each side of the grave, Theron, the tyrant of Agrigentum, shines the brighter.

He, the present victor, can trace descent through Ther-sandros, the son of Polyneices, who was son of Oedipos, to Cadmos, the first king of Thebes. It is a noble but not always fortunate line. Four instances of suffering that result in compensating glory are signaled out for our attention, and each example advances the meditation that will culmi-nate in Theron's curtailed apotheosis.

The colonists of Agrigentum, after great adversity, came to Sicily and founded Theron's city. They fulfilled what had been fated; they

> have come of age in wealth
> And the elegance that graced
> Their sterling excellence.

The meaning of their allotment, their share in alternating good and bad, will be clarified in the fourth or Oedipos-variation. Here, the poet contents himself with a simpler meditation, which is introduced as an abbreviated theme at the beginning of the variation, and reoccurs as a conclusion to the ring-structure that isolates the variation. The thought is straightforward: when good luck comes, we forget our previous history of pain. Melodic elements, however, that will receive elaboration later, are here first introduced: the prevalence of pain; an unjust act cannot be undone; not even Time can change the end result; god's special allotment, good fortune, tips the balance in our favor —a metaphor reminiscent perhaps of the scale Zeus holds in the *Iliad* to measure the lives of Hector and Achilles.

Variations 2 and 3 leap in retrograde chronology back to the two daughters of Cadmos, Semele and Ino, who are first introduced as the common subject and then given independent treatment. They are united not only by the paradigmatic meaning they share —both died, yet did not die; both escaped from Time to eternity— but also by the encircling meditation. It is introduced by a restatement of the balance-metaphor:

> Plummets pain,
> For happiness the victor rises!

and returns in more extended form as the poet attempts to see some metaphysical basis for the alternation in man's condition:

> Look you:
> Our end in death
> Is not determined —nor if this sun's
> Child, our day, we terminate
> At peace without reversal.
> Streams of joy,
> Streams of trouble come: mankind's tide.
> Moera —yes, she has

This family's good at heart, but with prosperity, their
   heritage
From god, she brings some suffering for time to turn
Upon them.

Following as it does upon the mythical examples of Semele
and Ino, who achieved immortality, the passage can only
mean that we do not know two things: whether when we
die we really die, and whether we shall be able to reach the
end of our lifetime without reversal (critics have usually
thought that the two statements were doublets for the same
idea, namely, that we do not know when we shall die). The
melodies—Time, the end, and Moera, or our allotment—
reoccur, the final one recalling the *Iliad*'s description of the
two urns that stand outside the gate of Zeus. The meaning
of the first variation's αἰὼν ... μόρσιμος ("they have come of
age" —or more literally, "their fated age") and θεοῦ μοῖρα
("god's Election" —or more literally, "god's allotment") is
now clarified. Man's condition requires that he receive a dispensation of both good and bad; Time will bring to pass the
change from happiness to pain, even though the god may
ordain the preponderance of pleasure.

   The meditation is incomplete, however, for the fourth
variation attempts to identify life's vicissitude with an ethical
principle: our life is predestined by a predestination that
we earn. The meditation that concluded the previous variation here functions as transition. Oedipos (the μόριμος υἱός,
or fated or fatal son) is the new mythic paradigm: he killed
his father, Laios, and "brought to pass/ The Pythic prophecy," which idea is signaled by verbal reminiscence
(τέλεσσεν) as a restatement of the end result (τέλος). The
meditation has thus determined the coloration of this narrative section. Indeed, it would not be too fanciful to see the
pessimistic ἐπί τι καὶ πῆμ'ἄγει ... (". . . she brings some suffering for time to turn/ Upon them") mirrored optimistically in
the victory-catalog by the verbal reminiscence ἄγαγον,

which completes the Oedipos-narrative: Theron emerges from the backdrop of the suffering of Oedipos' line with the compensating glory of his Olympic victory:

> For he, himself, at Olympia
> Took a prize; and at Pytho and the Isthmus, the Grace
> He shares with brother and coheir conferred the wreath
> For racing the twelve-lap
> Four-in-hand.

(We do not contend that verbal reminiscence is completely within the poet's control or plan, but merely that it signals what parts or visions he held counterpoised in his mind as he composed his ode. It is, of course, the despair of the translator that words are colored by the context and that mere literalness will catch the words but not the poem.) The meditation which concludes the fourth variation is so brilliant and extended that, like the chaconne of the second Bach violin partita, it seems, despite its close ties with its context, to free itself from the poem and stand alone as a song. It would, however, falsify the meaning were we not to see it as well as the conclusion to the preceding variations. Victory compensates for suffering. Such is the simple gnomic summary which marks the transition from Theron's victory-catalog to the vision of the life after death. The metaphor of the balance reoccurs:

> wealth
> Fine-wrought with excellence yields
> A mixture critical
> For joy and troubles, weighing down our wild anxieties.

The light begins to flow in.

The poet has found the key that will free us from the reversals of Time. Wealth, as he has said in other poems as well, allows his patron to bear vicissitude nobly, since he has a reserve of good to poise against the bad. This wealth is for Theron studded with excellence, however, which means, first, physical excellence, or victory in the games, but in the succeeding meditation it is colored with moral qualities. For wealth by itself can brave this world's disasters, but in the life to come, where sins are rewarded or punished, moral excellence alone is liberation from the cycles of reincarnation. It is the critical mixture by which we surpass the alternation of joy and troubles; "It is a star conspicuous, quintessential/ Human brilliance —." The sun's child, the day that we as humans cannot see through clearly to its end, is transformed by this star into a brightness stably shining in the afterworld in which the day's sun obliterates night. (The text is corrupt and has been much disputed; we suggest, however, that this meaning, which can be justified from the text, alone has relevance to the context of the poem.) This reward for the good is unfortunately only temporary; it is the reward for those who have done no wrong in this life. But the life after death is also a test in which we may do both good and bad —and evil there need not wait for death to earn its punishment, for those who sin in death are plunged immediately into inexpressible torment. Our existence, which in this world is governed by the amoral allotment of god —against which wealth alone can act as buffer— is in the afterlife governed entirely by moral principles. Such is the answer to the paradox which arises when, as Gilbert Murray has said, a people takes a natural force for its god, a power that of course refuses to abide by the ethical standards civilization evolves to govern man's activities. We work in this world for our livelihood, but success does not always meet our efforts. There, the good need not work:

> no land their hand's
> Strength turns,
> Nor churns it waters of the sea
> For poverty and emptiness.

Souls, after their trial in the afterlife, return again to this life and are again subject to vicissitude. Three times the cycle is completed. Those who can "wholly keep a soul inviolate" are given their final reward in eternity; they, like Semele and Ino, achieve a godlike state: they dwell in the Hesperides, the Islands of the Blest:

> Where flowers burn to gold:
> Or splendent trees or plants
> That water feeds;

where Cronos, in this realm of Rhadamanthys' equity, is revealed as the ethical god. He is given the epiphany that Zeus, because of his immoral narrative connotations, can never entirely achieve.

The passage closes with a simple catalog of a few who have reached the Hesperides:

> And Peleus is with them, and Cadmos, they say,
> And . . . .
> Achilles, who cast down Hector,
> Alas! Troy's most steadfast pillar; and Cycnos
> Brought to death; and the Aethiop, Dawn's son.

We see perhaps the final meaning of the balance-metaphor, not only in Rhadamanthys' realm of equity, but also in Achilles' reward.

Perhaps the catalog, had it been completed, would have promised the eventual inclusion of the patron, Theron. Such is, in any case, the implication in Pindar's break-off formula: he returns to the metaphor of the archer with which the ode had begun. His poem has three separate targets: a god, a hero, and a contemporary. The poet's task is to include all three, to place Theron in the company of Zeus and Heracles, but yet so to modulate his praise, his vaunt, that it may strike the correct measure of moderation. The phrase had been provisionally found in the claim that Theron, the bulwark of Agrigentum, was "his family's royal flowering in civic rectitude." The postlude, then, resumes the metaphor: the poet has many arrows that he might shoot, but he chooses to cur-

tail the catalog of the Blest, since if the poet does not observe
due measure, boredom will ensue —such is the cliché that we
have seen in other poems. It is given here, however, a novel
ornamentation. Pindar is the eagle, the bird of Zeus; the envious throng is transformed into crows. Ancient commen-
tators and many modern ones have identified these envious
people as the poets Simonides and his nephew Bacchylides,
but the personal reference, although exciting to the Hellenistic critics, would be in exceedingly bad taste; the force of
the cliché demands, moreover, that we see these others as
nothing more than the traditional danger, the envious throng.
Against the high flight of Pindar, against his transcendental
vaunt, their voices can chatter only words that have no meaning. The bow is aimed, the arrow shot toward Agrigentum,
and the praise that the poet sings is only an ornamentation of
the earlier phrase concerning Theron's civic rectitude:

> I swear in truth
> Our century has no city seen
> Give birth to man
> More philanthropic, of hand more open: who
> But Theron?

The poem ends with the simple conceit that the particulars of
Theron's eulogy, like grains of sand, escape enumeration.
But the praise has been sufficient for the cognoscenti, perhaps the initiates, the elect, who have already had the revelation of the cycles of reincarnation. The envious throng, which
cannot understand the vaunt, is left outside its meaning, with
nothing but the moderate eulogy about Theron's rectitude
and generosity at which to cavil.

The burden of the meditation, however, moves us to consider the praise that Pindar does not express. Theron is head
of a just city; the prominence of this city was seen as his ancestors' coming-of-age in wealth and excellence. It was their
allotment of good that compensated for bad. This same com-
bination of wealth and excellence was later shown to redeem

us from vicissitude on both sides of the grave. When the phrase is restated in the postlude, it confers on Theron the key to possible immortality. The archer's arrow in striking Theron will perhaps hit all three: a god, a hero, and a contemporary.

OLYMPIA II: For Theron of Agrigentum: Victory With Chariot

ΑΝΑΞΙΦΟΡΜΙΓΓΕΣ ΥΜΝΟΙ

PRELUDE

(strophe)
O Hymns whose king is Phorminx,
Which god acclaim, which hero, and which of our
    contemporaries?
Consider: Pisa pertains to Zeus; and the Olympics
Heracles inaugurated
As pick of his battle crop;
And Theron for the winning quadriga
Proclaim, our scrupulous host,
Bulwark of Agrigentum,
And his family's royal flowering in civic rectitude.

VARIATION 1

(antistrophe)
Great were their struggles in affliction
To gain this sacred river city: they were
The cynosure of Sicily, have come of age in wealth

Olympia II

And the elegance that graced
Their sterling excellence. O Rhea's
Son by Cronos, O Olympus-throned,
Enthroned at the Alpheos, at Contests'
Acme: warm
To my song; benevolent, entail them to their fathers' lands

(epode)

Through all their dynasty. *Of what*
Is done —just and unjust— undone not
The universal father, Time, might make the end result:
Yet . . . good fortune comes and we forget
Our chronic agonies, that, overwhelmed
In our rejoicing, die

(strophe)

When god's Election elevates
To towering felicity.

VARIATION 2

My proof is Cadmos' daughters
Royally ensconced —but after what extremities!
Plummets pain,
For happiness the victor rises!
With Olympians she lives who died
In thunder-crash —Semele (how reached
Her hair!). And Pallas
Loves her; and Zeus her Consort; and her son, the
ivy-emblemed.

VARIATION 3

(antistrophe)

There are legends, too, that in the sea
With Nereus' ocean daughters life immortal
Is Ino's lot for all of time. *Look you:*
Our end in death
Is not determined —nor if this sun's

Child, our day, we terminate
At peace without reversal.
Streams of joy,
Streams of trouble come: mankind's tide.

(epode)

Moera —yes, she has
This family's good at heart, but with prosperity, their
*   heritage*
From god, she brings some suffering for time to turn
Upon them:

VARIATION 4

the fatal son killed
Laios in his path and brought to pass
The Pythic prophecy.

(strophe)

She saw him, his knife-edged Erinys;
And set to internecine death his warring breed —
Bar extinction: Thersandros survived Polyneices'
Fall, to glory
Youthful in the Games and battle,
New growth reviving the Adrastid
Tree, from which root and seed
Aenesidamos' son —
No wonder of it— meets eulogy and lyres.

(antistrophe)

For he, himself, at Olympia
Took a prize; and at Pytho and the Isthmus, the Grace
He shares with brother and coheir conferred the wreath
For racing the twelve-lap
Four-in-hand. *Success emancipates*
Contestants from despair: wealth
Fine-wrought with excellence yields
A mixture critical
For joy and troubles, weighing down our wild anxieties;

Olympia II

(epode)

It is a star conspicuous, quintessential
Human brilliance —if he who has it could but know
The future! . . . that the dead whose souls are there
    malfeasant instantly
Pay retribution; and our sins, here, in this realm
Of Zeus: there is a judge beneath the earth
To sentence them, inexorable.

(strophe)

But sunlight perpetual: the nights
Are days; day night —they labor less,
Yet get their livelihood, the good: no land their hand's
Strength turns,
Nor churns it waters of the sea
For poverty and emptiness. No,
Who kept their faith are given
Life —not tears—
With god's Elect. (Those others? See not their torment!)

(antistrophe)

And if three times each side
The grave these wholly keep a soul inviolate,
They come at last on Zeus's road to Cronos'
Citadel: where ocean
Airs ensweep Hesperides;
Where flowers burn to gold:
Or splendent trees or plants
That water feeds.
With these they wreathe their hands, weave crowns

(epode)

In Rhadamanthys' realm of equity,
Judge delegate on the right of our Lord the Father,
Who shares as royal consort Rhea's high-sovereign throne.
And Peleus is with them, and Cadmos, they say,

And Achilles —for Zeus's heart had heard
The mother's supplication—

(strophe)

Achilles, who cast down Hector,
Alas! Troy's most steadfast pillar; and Cycnos
Brought to death; and the Aethiop, Dawn's son.

POSTLUDE

Many and sharp
The arrows in the quiver beneath my arm
That speak to cognoscenti: the vulgar
Want interpreters. For the poet's
Knowledge is innate;
Tyros, you furioso crows, croak on: I

(antistrophe)

Am the sacred bird of Zeus.
Up, heart! take aim to target! Whom
Wound —shoot gently, mind!— this time
With glory's arrows?
Toward Agrigentum: draw the string;
Sing. I swear in truth
Our century has no city seen
Give birth to man
More philanthropic, of hand more open: who

(epode)

But Theron? Enough! or excess
Will trample praise —not with reason, but men
Are rabid; they want to hide in verbiage a noble's high
Achievements. The sand escapes enumeration.
And he ... how many joys conferred on others,
Who might tell?

PYTHIA II: Introduction and Credentials

The interpretation of the four odes Pindar composed for king Hieron of Syracuse has been colored by the belief, first suggested by the ancient Hellenistic scholars, that Pindar eventually came to a falling-out with his patron and that the poet Bacchylides, who is known to have been employed at the Syracusan court, was instrumental in instigating the rupture. This preconceived idea has been used to establish the chronological sequence of the Hieron odes, for only two of them are securely dated —"Olympia I," assigned to the year 476 B.C., and usually considered the first poem, written when Pindar was himself at the court being entertained by his patron; and "Pythia I," assigned to the year 470 B.C., with Pindar apparently back in Greece. The remaining two odes, "Pythia II" and "Pythia III," make no reference to a specific athletic event, and therefore could not be dated by the ancient scholars, who had at their disposal the complete record of victories at Olympia and Delphi. Most scholars have seen "Pythia II" as a direct apologia of the poet to his patron, in which he cuts through court-circles and offers a proud justification of his own integrity in answer to his supposed Syracusan calumniators. It has even been suggested that the occasion for the poem was Hieron's Olympic victory of 468 B.C., for which Bacchylides' *III* is the official poem, and that Pindar, who had not received the commission for this important event, composed this ode on his own initiative. "Pythia II," however, mentions that the poet is going to send another poem after the present one; such would indicate, probably, that he was still on good enough terms with his patron.

We do not wish to labor a scholarly point in this essay, but it will be seen that the dating of "Pythia II" is extremely important for an understanding of what this most difficult ode means. For example, are the concluding statements about slander really a reference to the supposed quarrel? Or are they merely, as we shall argue, highly imaginative elaborations of an epinician cliché? The question is valid because it is solely on the riddling language of this poem that the belief in the falling-out is based. The belief has been read back into the other Hieron odes as well; but without the preconceived expectation, none of these other passages could stand as evidence.

There is one item of evidence, however, which establishes a date before which "Pythia II" could not have been written. The poem mentions the gratitude of the people of Western Locris for a benefit they have received from Hieron: Anaxilas of Rhegium had threatened them with war, and Hieron, in the year 477 B.C., had exerted his influence to protect them. The poem must have been written, therefore, sometime after 477 B.C.; since Hieron died in 467 B.C., the poem obviously must be placed somewhere in this decade. Since, by the traditional interpretation, the poet could not have argued with his patron before he got to know him, the poem is placed toward the end of the decade. The Western Locrian affair is, however, a somewhat minor event in Hieron's career; and we might expect that a mention of it, especially a mention not in the context of an extensive catalog of his acts, should normally follow close upon the event. Such, no doubt, would have been the unanimous conclusion

—it was Gaspar's, for example— had it not been for the misinterpretation of the ode's final section.

The mention of the two odes that Pindar says in "Pythia II" he is sending his patron may help us to make more precise the occasion for this poem:

This poem like Phoenician ware I send you
Over the grey sea;
May it be your pleasure to await a second poem, in
    Aeolic meter,
The Castorian epinician ode,
The glory of the seven-stringed lyre.

The first poem is obviously "Pythia II," itself; that it is sent "like Phoenician ware" perhaps indicates only that it is shipped off like export-goods, a variation on Pindar's customary metaphor confusing the celebration performance and the voyage by which it travels from the poet to his patron. If the second poem was ever written and if it is still extant, it can be only "Olympia I," which is an epinician ode in Aeolic meter, written, as "Castorian" apparently implies, to commemorate a victory with horse, either single or harnessed in a team. "Pythia II," therefore, must have been written in the year 477 B.C., or at least before the poet's arrival in Syracuse for the festivities attendant on Hieron's Olympic success. Consequently, it is the first of the Hieron odes, and not the last. The chronology of the other odes offers no objection: "Pythia I," which mentions Hieron's illness, would be the third in the sequence; and "Pythia III," written apparently upon receipt of the news of Hieron's approaching death, would be the last. Both "Pythia I" and "III" show greater intimacy and understanding of the patron, whereas "Olympia I" is more formally brilliant and "Pythia II" speaks mainly of the poet himself.

It is hard, no doubt, for someone who does not know Greek to understand how the same words can be open to such divergent interpretation. The cause of this amazing disagreement is to be sought in the nature of Pindar's language itself, which plays extreme variations on simple, nearly stable ideas. The entire set, as it were, of variations describes the poet's meaning; too often, however, one variation in isolation catches the critic's attention, and he attempts to attach the language to some referent in reality, thereby doing violence to the other variations in the set. We shall see, for example, that in this poem the poet says, "Be what you know you are"; the meaning is clear in context; the critic who takes it out of context or who imports into the poem for a context real everyday Syracusan living sees the statement as a rebuke addressed to the patron, however unlikely such matter may seem for the given epinician genre. It will be our task to establish the organic life of the poem.

The statement comes at a pivotal point in the poem: the ode proper has seemingly ended with a typical sign-off formula, and a somewhat asymmetrical coda-like appendage now spells out for the poet the implications of what he has just finished saying. Because of the difficulty of this ode, we shall indulge in a somewhat more complete analysis of the transitions in the poet's thought than has been our custom in other essays; the coda can be understood only as it plays its comment upon the first part of the poem.

The opening invocation to the city of Syracuse is remarkable not only for the brilliance of its language but also for the obscurity caused by what it does *not* say. The city is great, a union of four separate towns; it is famous for its power in war and for the fine line of horses that is bred there. The poet identifies himself as Theban and announces that the victory has been with chariot and team of four horses and that Hieron, in his triumph, has dedicated, on the island of Ortygia, which is the site of his palace, the trophies he has won. Ortygia is characterized, because of the spring Arethousa, as sacred to Artemis, who has been Hieron's benefactress in taming the horses. What is missing, of course, is any information that might identify the particular game or games that have been won. Instead of that, the antistrophe offers a general condition, which claims that because Hieron is dear to Artemis and Hermes, he will win whenever his breed of horses runs. Poseidon too, apparently because of his connection with horses, will oversee Hieron's victory. There is no return in this fairly long ode to the subject of the victory, although we might have expected the particularizing information to have been added at the end of the poem. We have only the general condition, and, since we are not the contemporary audience, who would have known, must guess at its significance. Or do we indeed have a return of a kind in the promised Castorian epinician ode? That is to say, the generalized condition is answered by a victory not yet won and a poem still to be written.

The idea of a victory, though yet to come, entails a cliché of the genre: triumph demands payment in eulogy. Pindar broaches the theme by saying that various kings have been recipients of such panegyric:

> For other kings
> Another has composed resounding hymns in payment for
>   their excellence.

He then proceeds to list examples: Cinyras, whom the people of Cyprus praise, and Hieron, who has won the gratitude of a woman from Western Locris. Through these two examples, however, he has modulated to a rephrasing of the cliché: these kings conferred benefits, and the praise they receive stems from the gratefulness they have elicited. It is in illustration of this rephrased idea that the third example, that of Ixion, is introduced:

> By divine ordinance Ixion too, they say, proclaims to
>   men
> This moral, on winged wheel
> In all ways whirled:

The benefactor one must greet
With shining recompense.

The example of Ixion receives extended narrative elaboration: he is, however, a different kind of example than Cinyras and Hieron, for he is the negative illustration —he is the one who has not paid his benefactor. For the benefactor this time was Zeus, who welcomed Ixion to Olympus only to find that Ixion attempted to seduce Hera, a signal example of ingratitude, which was met by a signal punishment— his eternal repetition of his own story's moral as he whirls through time bound to the spokes of a wheel. His story, moreover, is punctuated by a variation on the Delphic homily, "Know thyself," which meant probably, "Know the limitations of your station or condition":

See your measure in what you are.

Ixion's deluded aspirations are countered by a delusion contrived by Zeus, a hallucination that only seemed to be Hera; it was with this vaporous nothing that the adultery was committed; and the offspring of the union present a refinement on the wheel-torture, for Ixion bred a line of monsters. The narrative ends with a magnificent hymn to the deity who has such power:

God's expectation fulfills his every plan,
God, who overtakes the eagle in its flight and leaves
The dolphin swimming
Far behind, who bends the arrogant down
And ageless fame to others grants.

At this point, halfway through the poem, the poet begins to speak of his own obligation; he has, however, by the myth, elevated Zeus to the position of the third example in his benefactor-catalog, and the poet is therefore forced to see himself as a possible Ixion, should he not meet the requirements of his obligation to eulogize. To show his consciousness of his possible role, Pindar plays upon himself the figure of a poet who was indeed an Ixion, Archilochos, the poet who so violently satirized an enemy that the man was said to have killed himself. Such reviling poetry upsets the reciprocal benefit-system that should pertain between poet and patron, and Archilochos in consequence lived a life of poverty:

> For I see across the years in utter poverty
> Archilochos, the satirist, grown fat on his words rich
> In hate.

Pindar blots out his Archilochos persona by a proud restatement of the proper theme for poetry, the person who has wealth and is blessed with good luck:

> Wealth and fortune's gifts
> Are theme for poetry.

It is thus that he flees the imagined danger that he might indulge in "slander's insatiate bite." There hovers in the background, of course, a certain ambiguity, for the one who bites is bitten, and the satirist receives no benefits from his patron, but dies in poverty.

If in the parallelism of paradigms Pindar had met and avoided his role as Ixion, the other half of the comparison is implied in the placement of Hieron in the hieratic pose that balances him with the superlative power of Zeus or god. Hieron indeed is the proper subject for eulogy, for he is opulent, and king of a multitude. In the actual phrasing of his praise Pindar assumes a defensive attitude, which seems to protect his patron from the danger of the disparagement that the poet has just so skillfully suppressed; he thereby can word the eulogy more extravagantly without encountering a critic's charge that he but flatters:

> Should someone
> Claim your opulence and glory have been surpassed
> In Greece, that other men before were greater,
> His empty mind grapples with nothingness.

The Archilochean persona, as it grapples with nothingness, now recalls Ixion, hallucinated in the cloud's embrace, that "man deluded who lusted for a cloud's embrace/ And chased hallucination's sweet lie." The cliché in which the poet attempts to avoid the charge of excessive praise or flattery forms the armature on which Pindar builds the particularizing panegyric of Hieron; Hieron was a great general in his youth but his maturer activities as governor of a city are so magnificent that no praise would be too extravagant:

> But your maturer
> Counsels negate all risk another say
> I praise too much.

By a most subtle juxtaposition and modulation of paradigms, Pindar has paid in full his eulogistic debt; he has avoided various imagined dangers in his course and thereby makes the final accolade the more secure and convincing. The eulogistic ode presents a problem of focusing, as the poet directs all attention away from a variety of distracting reflectors and plays the gathered light full upon the extolled recipient. Everything else acts as a foil against which is placed the final nucleus of panegyric. It is the proclamation that the poet promised at the beginning of the ode, and he returns again to a more ornate treatment of the voyage from Thebes to Syracuse:

> A proud ship wreathed with flowers shall I board in
>   celebration
> Of your excellence.

The poem is given its envoi and the patron is directed to await a second poem, which will hymn the particularized victory that this ode lacks.

The coda begins, as we have said, with the statement, "Be what you know you are." It should be clear now, however, that this is another version of the "Know thyself" homily which had been referred to Ixion's condition. Since Ixion, when applied to the realm of poetry, became Archilochos, or Pindar's negative persona, we should expect that the present statement also applies to the poet. As such, it introduces Pindar as the subject of the asymmetrical conclusion.

The language is enigmatic, a rapid shifting of personae, which seems, at least in part, a parody on the style of Archilochos. Pindar is not a monkey to delight a child; he is Rhadamanthys, the incorruptible judge of souls in the afterlife:

A fine thing
Is a monkey —fine for children; but Rhadamanthys thrives,
Harvesting the fruit of thought's perfection: his heart
Unswerving avoids
Inequity.

He modulates again to the negative as he speaks of the whispered calumnies that Rhadamanthys, like Pindar before, avoids; and he appears this time in a beast-figuration. He is not the fox, who, like Archilochos, dies in poverty for all his stratagems:

... these purveyors of slander, like foxes
Constant in their hate. What does the fox profit by
    his foxing?
Nothing!

Again a staccato modulation, and Pindar reemerges as a cork, a fishing-float that cannot be sunk despite the downward pull of the net:

For I am the cork above the net: the rest
Works in the sea-depths; but I float
High and dry.

By a new shift to the negative, he gives definite form to the Archilochean persona, which becomes an imagined commoner who attempts to detract from the eulogy which is

Hieron's due; the commoner becomes a dog and recalls the mythological paradigm of Ixion and his phantom love:

> The commoner, for all his guile, can wield no influence
> Among the nobles: nonetheless forever fawning
> He weaves delusion —
> For himself.

By an assertive claim to the positive role, Pindar is transformed into the wolf and thus climactically incorporates the Archilochean beast-fable to the service of his own persona; he can now ascribe to himself both eulogy and hate-poetry: eulogy repays his benefactor, and hate-poetry destroys his benefactor's enemies, and therefore also meets his obligation to his patron:

> I share not his audacity. To a friend,
> Be friendly; a wolf-like enemy, I will run
> The enemy down, treading my devious
> Paths.

The wording in the final clause, moreover, recalls the figure which had been used to introduce the whole section on the benefactors and their repayment, beginning with Cinyras.

Such a gathering of beasts perhaps corresponds to the breed of monsters that was sired by Ixion; Pindar's final assumption of an animal role defeats by assimilation his alter ego. The Centaurs that were born in the second generation from the adulterous union are, of course, the exact opposite of the fine breed of racehorses that come from Hieron's stable.

Pindar next places at his patron's disposal the powers of his poetry and seems to indicate that although he is new to the society of a monarch he will not fail to succeed:

> In all societies the out-spoken man succeeds —
> In monarchies, in democracy's clamorous throng, or
>   when wise
> Oligarchs guard the city.

Pythia II

The mention of the various types of government induces a treatment of the vicissitude cliché:

> Fight
> Not with god,
> Who lifts up now the one estate, now
> To another grants great glory.

This passage is followed by a return to the theme of slander, and therefore presents the same pattern that had occurred at the end of the Ixion myth. We have seen that god in the first occurrence was replaced by Hieron, as the poet met his obligation. Here then, by juxtaposition, Hieron's estate, although subject to normal vicissitude and the cycles of governmental change, is somewhat secure; Pindar cannot falsify the nature of the universe, but Hieron's wealth, it is implied, is adequately stable. The calumniators, who had been modulated in the preceding passage to fawning flatterers, cannot accept god's pattern of order. They now become for a moment the positive personae, but of course fail in their naïveté to strike the true tone of eulogy. The Delphic homily repeats with reference to them; they are surveyors, staking out a property, but in their stupidity they measure out too much and implant the stake in their own hearts:

> Cold
> Comfort for envious minds! They stretch the line
> Beyond its measure and stake
> Their claim —in their hearts! A painful property
> Is all that they surveyed.

The poet therefore has returned to the "Be what you know you are" statement with which the coda had begun, and in his meditation he has explored what indeed his function is. He accepts, as he for one last time suffers transformation, the burden of a world in change, against which he must orchestrate his panegyric; he refuses to fight with god and hopes that the poems he writes will please his patron:

> Take up the yoke and bear it lightly on your neck:
>   that's the right
> Way. To kick against
> The pricks —a slippery path
> For poetry. May I live with nobles
> And please them nobly.

It is a dangerous procedure first to assume, on the basis of no evidence, a biographical situation for a work of art, and then to force the work to conform to this preconceived hunch. Even when the biography is well known, the procedure is somewhat inapposite. Now that we have dated the poem to a particular year and have examined the nature of its communication, however, it might be of some interest for us to hazard a guess about the situation for which such a poem might have been written. What is said can be but conjecture, although perhaps a probable conjecture. We see Pindar still in Greece, approached by an envoy from Hieron and asked to accept the highly honorific commission of the Olympic ode that would celebrate Hieron's victory, should he actually win. It is perhaps significant that none of the extant Olympic odes precedes this date. Pindar signals his acceptance by the writing of an ode that treats in summary fashion Hieron's earlier victories at lesser games and holds out the expectation that the major ode will be written. Moreover, in a scherzo rhythm, he exhibits his virtuosity as he meditates on his function as eulogistic poet. The jeu d'esprit in which he, as it were, displays his wares, is, by its extravagance, the cause of the ode's near incomprehensibility; it is a sample-piece in many styles. "Pythia II," therefore, would be meant to precede Pindar's arrival in Syracuse and to act as an introduction in which he presents his own credentials.

Pythia II: For Hieron of Syracuse:
For Victories Past and Future

ΜΕΓΑΛΟΠΟΛΙΕΣ Ω ΣΤΡΑΚΟΣΑΙ ΒΑΘΤΠΟΛΕΜΟΤ

STROPHE

Great, O Syracuse, among the cities, war-plunged
Ares' precinct, and of men and their horses in caparison
The divine nurse:
To you this song from lustrous Thebes I bear,
This proclamation of the harnessed four, their earth-shaking
    hoofs
And the chariot victory when Hieron triumphant
Bound the island of Ortygia in wreaths afar resplendent,
This royal seat of Artemis, lady of rivers, by whose aid
His taming hands those dapple-reined
Colts broke.

ANTISTROPHE

In his two hands, she whose delight is arrows,
And Hermes, guardian of the games, place honor
Shining, should ever
He yoke the horses' strength to polished chariots

137

Obedient to the bridle, the while invoking trident's
Wide-dominioned brandisher. For other kings
Another has composed resounding hymns in payment for
    their excellence:
Cypriote voices often swirl about the name of Cinyras,
Aphrodite's chosen priest, the beloved
Pre-eminent of Apollo

EPODE

The golden-haired. What motive leads them is reverent
Gratitude, the reward for benefits. And to you no less,
Deinomenes' son, the woman from western Locris
At her door sings praise
From out war's tribulations ineluctable
Now looking, by your efforts saved.
By divine ordinance Ixion too, they say, proclaims to men
This moral, on winged wheel
In all ways whirled:
The benefactor one must greet
With shining recompense.

STROPHE

He learned his lesson. Graciously received by Cronos'
Sons he led a life of ease, but long
Could not endure
Prosperity: it drove him mad and he aspired to the love
Of Hera, whom Zeus's sumptuous bed possessed.
Behold, presumption goaded him to haughty
Ruin: mere man he suffered what he merited, his special tor-
    ture.
Two penal offenses bore their fruit: he first
Taught mortals murder, by kindred
Blood contaminate;

ANTISTROPHE

Moreover, in the vast seclusion of royal chambers,
He attempted Zeus's wife. See your measure
In what you are.

Pythia II

A strange adultery cast to utter ruin
This man deluded who lusted for a cloud's embrace
And chased hallucination's sweet lie:
Mere form, a shape that seemed the sovereign daughter
Of Uranian Cronos; she was the trap the hands of Zeus
Had set —exquisite torment! He made
The four-spoked prison

EPODE

His destruction: bound in shackles that defy escape,
Ixion manifests a message for all to share.
No Graces in attendance when she bore —mother unique—
His unique and lusty son,
Rejected from society by gods and men.
She raised him, named him Centaur.
He coupled with Magnesian mares roaming the foothills of
    Mount Pelion,
And sired a breed astounding
That looked like both its parents:
The mother below the waist;
Above, the father.

STROPHE

God's expectation fulfills his every plan,
God, who overtakes the eagle in its flight and leaves
The dolphin swimming
Far behind, who bends the arrogant down
And ageless fame to others grants. My obligation:
To flee slander's insatiate bite.
For I see across the years in utter poverty
Archilochos, the satirist, grown fat on his words rich
In hate. Wealth and fortune's gifts
Are theme for poetry:

ANTISTROPHE

Your riches, Prince, are manifest; your spirit liberal,
Lord of the tower-crowned citadel and its multitude.
Should someone

Claim your opulence and glory have been surpassed
In Greece, that other men before were greater,
His empty mind grapples with nothingness.
A proud ship wreathed with flowers shall I board in
    celebration
Of your excellence. In youth stoutheartedness in war's ordeal
    avails:
There it was, I say, you found
Your boundless fame,

EPODE

There amidst the men who spurred their horses,
Or there contending with the infantry. But your maturer
Counsels negate all risk another say
I praise too much. Farewell:
This poem like Phoenician ware I send you
Over the grey sea;
May it be your pleasure to await a second poem, in Aeolic
    meter,
The Castorian epinician ode,
The glory of the seven-stringed lyre.

Coda

Be what you know you are.
A fine thing

STROPHE

Is a monkey —fine for children; but Rhadamanthys thrives,
Harvesting the fruit of thought's perfection: his heart
Unswerving avoids
Inequity, the inevitable sequel if a man traffics
In whispered calumnies. For both parties, an evil
Irreparable, these purveyors of slander, like foxes
Constant in their hate. What does the fox profit by his foxing?
Nothing! For I am the cork above the net: the rest
Works in the sea-depths; but I float
High and dry.

Pythia II

The commoner, for all his guile, can wield no influence
Among the nobles: nonetheless forever fawning
He weaves delusion —
For himself. I share not his audacity. To a friend,
Be friendly; a wolf-like enemy, I will run
The enemy down, treading my devious
Paths. In all societies the out-spoken man succeeds —
In monarchies, in democracy's clamorous throng, or when
   wise
Oligarchs guard the city. Fight
Not with god,

EPODE

Who lifts up now the one estate, now
To another grants great glory. Cold
Comfort for envious minds! They stretch the line
Beyond its measure and stake
Their claim —in their hearts! A painful property
Is all that they surveyed.
Take up the yoke and bear it lightly on your neck: that's the
   right
Way. To kick against
The pricks —a slippery path
For poetry. May I live with nobles
And please them nobly.

OLYMPIA I: The Hierarchies of Fire

A fire burns in the night, and the fire is not fire, but gold, which, among the standards of wealth, is prince. It is thus that vision and word merge in the poet's mind so that the gold shines in the night and fire is wealth. The sentence in Greek begins with a simple apposition, the stark equation of gold and fire; what follows does not attenuate the figure, but, in the guise of explanation, further imbricates, for the night is appropriate to the fire, whereas proud wealth, which shares the same verb as fire, must be the category of which fire is example. Most literally, we might translate: "Gold, burning fire: let me explain: it is clearly seen at night beyond proud wealth"— except that, in the Greek, "let me explain" is only an adverbial relative, and the subject "it" is unexpressed. We see the gold itself on fire, burning perhaps like some mountain beacon that outshines the other tokens of wealth.

Although gold has supreme rank in the family of elements that signal man's riches, it has a position lower than water, which, inasmuch as it clearly undergoes transformation into mist and ice, was considered by the philosophers the highest stuff in the hierarchy of primordial elements: water, fire, air, earth. It was with the statement of this primacy that the poem began. And perhaps the fiery aura of gold is at least partially a carry-over from Pindar's meditation on the philosophers' truth. Fire in any case is uppermost in his mind as he moves on to his third category, that of the Greek national games. Here Olympia is the sun, the day fire, more brilliant than the other stars. Now both fire and air lend glory, and the athletic contest is similarly inextricable from the terms of the comparison:

> But be it victory
> Prize that you would chant, my heart,
> No further look than sun
> For shining star in day
> More conflagrant through empty empyrean.

Order, a series of three hierarchies, has been imposed on vision, but the clarity of what was seen transcends categorical expression. The descending series —primordial elements, riches, games— is counteracted by the ascendancy of fire, which moves from a lesser primordial element to the night-fire which accompanies lord wealth to, finally, the day-star that shines at Olympia. As fire gains ascendancy, language more lovingly envelops it. Water's supremacy is stated as an uncontestable truth: its function, like the Biblical texts in Taylor's poetry, is to establish the aria, whereas each of the two succeeding statements presents increasingly elaborate ornamentations until we, with Pindar, see the blazing noon of contest at Olympia. It was no doubt this brilliance of Olympia's connotations that refused to be conquered by the poet's schematization. The complex interaction of incipient rational order and the "presentational" Gestalt reflects Pindar's place in the development of the Western world's modes of thought. His mind still functions in terms of the archaic total vision —the immediate leap the oral bard could make from the particulars of reality to the generic type-scenes which could be communicated by his formulized mnemonically-oriented language. Particular reality is thus a child of the generic. Rational order will reverse the process and the generic will be simplified from the particular. The philosophic statement about primordial elements owes much, of course, to the archaic unconscious conviction of order, but it is an early step in inductive reasoning. Pindar founds his poem on this new pattern, but he is anachronistically conservative, a man who has himself seen the gods and whose ultimate truth is the transcendental hallucination of the Pythian priestess. Pindar's is the poetry of confident hesitation, a poetry in which metaphorical fire is too real, too present to the mind, for subjugation into the genera of thought.

The theme of hierarchies, reduced, at the end of the ode, to a gnomic utterance, turns the ode back to its opening motif: "... we all have each our greatness." The experience of the poem itself, however, has imposed new meaning. The ultimate is now the king's crown, and the injunction: "... search no further ..." unmistakably recalls the phrase at the beginning: "No further look than sun. ..." Hieron who will "walk this while the heights" is granted momentary epiphany with the attributes of the sun itself. He is this earlier Roi-Soleil. Or is he, since he has won, himself Olympia, for the poet can find no better game to sing, no better victor? In this sunburst of glory, in these cosmic heights, the poet moves, casting radiance on his patron who now, of course, a lesser luminary, owes his own light to the fire of the poet's homage. We have light brighter than the sun, a light which is source of all light, *saint langage,* as Valéry names it.

This Hieron-poem is, as the ancient scholiasts noted, actually a poem in praise of Pindar himself. The Pelops myth, ostensibly apposite both in that Syracuse is a Dorian colony and that Pelops' contest with Oenomaos set the precedent for the Olympic games, really has little to do with Hieron personally, whose wealth and kingship culminate in his function as patron:

Who sways his righteous scepter in Sicily, the orchard apple-

Rich, culling the buds of every excellence
And with especial radiance
Glorifies the flower of music.

The myth is at once both pyrotechnics and a proud credo
of the high function of poetry: the revolting story of Tantalos'
picnic in which his son, Pelops, was offered as food for the
gods, is no sooner broached than the poet rejects it in disgust
for a more culturally acceptable version in which Pelops is
the beloved of Poseidon. The poet thus in *recusatio* tells us
two stories. In the time-honored Hesiodic tradition, he cov-
ers his awareness of the divergence of myths by claiming that
other poets lie:

Men leave truth behind
When poetry bedecked with tinkling lies misleads them.
Why not? Her charm, which fashions fineness, ennobling all
That we esteem, contrives that incredulities too often
Seem quite credible.

The inference is obvious. Pindar offers not only the accouterments of poetry, its words and rhythms, but also the basic
structure of reality, truth like the philosophers' doctrine of
water's primacy. Pelops, ravished to the gods, must, in payment for his father's Promethean sin, his theft of ambrosia
and nectar, again return to live among mortals; his triumph
at Olympia was what he won to compensate for his ephemeral existence, for his relics there enshrined gain him the
honor of a saint. Hieron, too, must pass away: his existence
on the heights is transitory. If he wins again, the poet will
again sing his eulogy. But a lying eulogy finds refutation in
the passage of time; eulogy that dies is cold comfort. It is
Pindar's truth displayed not only in the correction of myth
but also in his reluctance to falsify Hieron's vulnerability
that gives the poet the right to walk on high, and justifies his
claim to the title of "poet paramount through all of Greece."
Thus fire's ascension, this mystic Bergsonian intuition, transcends the Cartesian coordinates.

OLYMPIA I: For Hieron of Syracuse: Victory With the Racehorse Pherenicos

---

ΑΡΙΣΤΟΝ ΜΕΝ ΥΔΩΡ Ο ΔΕ ΧΡΥΣΟΣ ΑΙΘΟΜΕΝΟΝ ΠΥΡ

STROPHE

Elements' prince is Water; and Gold ablaze night-
Fire outshines its lesser lords of wealth.
But be it victory
Prize that you would chant, my heart,
No further look than sun
For shining star in day
More conflagrant through empty empyrean —
Olympia: no Game more fine shall we ever sing.
What ode so celebrous enweaves
A poet's fancy as to cascade praise
Of Cronos' son here at Hieron's
Hearth, so blessed, so opulent,

ANTISTROPHE

Who sways his righteous scepter in Sicily, the orchard apple-
Rich, culling the buds of every excellence
And with especial radiance

Olympia I

Glorifies the flower of music
We play, symposiasts
Who frequent his banquet table.
Come —the Doric lyre, lift
It down: have not Pisa and Pherenicos' beauty
Inspired your mind's most sweet
Conceptions, when in the track at Alpheos
He yielded flanks unspurred: he raced
And joined to mastery his master,

EPODE

King of Syracuse and horsemanship, whose glory effulges
    here
A noble throng, this colony of Pelops the Lydian !
Pelops —whom Earth's Foundation, Poseidon
Most powerful, loved, when from the cauldron Clotho
    purified
He stepped with shoulder's ivory blazonry.
Ah, wonders never cease!
Men leave truth behind
When poetry bedecked with tinkling lies misleads them.

STROPHE

Why not? Her charm, which fashions fineness, ennobling all
That we esteem, contrives that incredulities too often
Seem quite credible—
But transitory: for days to come
Bear witness more reliable.
The safer path befits
Our mortal role: to eulogize divinity.
Therefore, O son of Tantalos, I shall oppose tradition:
Irreproachably they banqueted, those gods
Your father had invited to picnic at your Sipylos
Estates, with each one sharing what he had brought;
Then Trident —O Radiance!— abducted you

ANTISTROPHE

And lost his mind to passion, transporting you on mares of
     gold
To high supremely sovereign Zeus's mansion.
(There in other
Times came Ganymede
To satisfy this need in Zeus.)
You disappeared; your mother's searching-party
Failed at length to bring you back;
Then some jealous neighbor whispered: "Water
On fire was set to vigorous
Boil; limb by limb they butchered him;
To table served remains of flesh;
They portioned him round and ate."

EPODE

Impossible! I will not say the gods are gluttonous —no!
History proves that slander gets no profit.
If any man the watch-lords of Olympus
Have esteemed, that man was Tantalos; but stomach his
     great prosperity —
He could not. From luxury he caught insanity
That ruined him: our Father's massive
Rock hangs over him;
In struggling to free his head, he but wanders from felicity.

STROPHE

No hand can help this life he has of steadfast torment,
A torture merely last of four: "Whereas
He has robbed divinity
And given his drinking cronies
Our nectar and ambrosia, wherewith
We made him deathless. . . ." If man
Expects to sin unseen by god,
A sad mistake! Therefore the immortals abandoned
His son to the short-lived race

Olympia I

Of men. He grew to flower; the down
Had covered his chin black, when he bethought
Himself of the marriage a father

ANTISTROPHE

In Pisa advertised: his eminent, illustrious Hippodameia. To
    the shore
He went, the froth-white sea, alone, at dusk-dark;
And called on crashing
Surf: "O Lord of Trident!"
Who, incarnate then
Beside him, was addressed: "Our gifts
Of love from Cypris —come, Poseidon!—
If ever they roused your pleasure, shackle the bronze
Of Oenomaos' spear; chariot me
Most swift at Elis; make mastery
Mine: thirteen suitors already
Killed, he still postpones

EPODE

His daughter's marriage. High adventure picks no weakling.
Why would we who all must die loll
In shadows, nameless, vainly busy
With senile age, our chance for glory squandered? No!
My challenge is before me; grant me my success!"
Thus the words he handled
So effectively. God splendored him:
Chariot of gold, winged horses weariless.

STROPHE

Oenomaos' life he took —and the girl for his bed-mate: who
    bore
Him princes, six sons who quested excellence.
Now are mingled
With shining sacrificial blood
His venerated relics ensepulchered,
Where, near the pilgrims' altar,

Is the ford on Alpheos. Afar it flashes,
The fame from games Olympic, from Pelops' course,
Where fleetness of foot is contest,
And the zenith of strength's bold endurance.
Who triumphs has, for the rest of his life,
The honey of halcyon days:

ANTISTROPHE

He has won! But man's supremest good comes always
In present joy: his coronal that I must weave
In mode Equestrian
To rhythm Aeolic. This
I affirm: no friend and patron
At once both connoisseur
Of beauty and so prestigious lord
Of his contemporaries shall vestiture with robes of song
    adorn.
A god is guardian, Hieron,
With this injunction: to foster your affairs.
Provided he continue by your side, I hope
With swiftest chariot to celebrate

EPODE

What benefic road more sweet I find for words,
Returning where the hill of Cronos looms.
My Muse in zealous tendance has
Her strongest arrow; we all have each our greatness: the
    ultimate
Is crowned in kings. So search no further!
Be it yours to walk this while
The heights and mine to company
The victors, their poet paramount through all of Greece.

Pythia I: "So Is It in the Music of Men's Lives"

The poet stands, holds aloft his lyre, bathed now in the golden aura of its divine possessors, Apollo and the Muses. The jumbled banquet speech subsides and in the silence is struck the first sweep of notes, which spread, imposing their harmony and their rhythm on surrounding space. The tempo is first felt, in this musical prelude, then seen as the chorus begins to mold its body to the dictates of the lyre and to the words in meter the poet sings:

> Behold the gold, this lyre: you, Apollo's wealth in common
> With the Muses (their hair inwoven violet): harkens
> Dance, the source of festival, while
> Poets yield to rhythms
> You so finely flashing
> Fashion, yours the step in prelude
> To the chorus. . . .

The real lyre, visible to the poet and his audience, has perceptibly brought an order to the haphazard elements of surrounding life. Its attributes expand to cosmic significance; the real becomes a symbol, a transformation that is perhaps possible for the late archaic poet only because the real is still constantly present throughout the ensuing metamorphoses. The symbolic lyre is not a gratuitous poetic invention, but a concrete image which has struck metaphysical reverberations. Thus the opening invocation of the poem Pindar wrote for Hieron's Pythian victory passes on from the real to its wider significance, and the lyre quenches a fire which is at once both the lightning bolt of Zeus and the burning lava-flows of the erupting Aetna. The music is heard in heaven; and the war-god function of Zeus, the eagle, sleeps, charmed by the rhythmic waves. The image is redefined in a typical doublet-treatment: Ares, the god of war, sleeps, and the only arrows that fly are the bolts of melody:

> —you who quench the lightning's spear
> Of ever-flowing fire: sleeps
> The eagle, swift wings folded,
> Upon the staff of Zeus,
> His sovereign bird, and black the face of cloud, sweet
>   prisoning
> Of sight, you poured, enshrouding curve-beaked head:
> His back, in slumber, ripples liquid,
> Possessed by measured surge —
> Violent Ares, his sharp
> Spears' edge abandoned, here
> Relents, entranced. Yours the arrows now
> That stun the minds of gods:
> Of Leto's son this art, and Muses
> Robed in flowing folds.

The passage concludes with a return to Apollo and the Muses, and with the transcendence of the poet whose art makes the lyre sing. At the end of "Olympia I," Pindar had invited Hieron to walk with him on the heights; here, by the alchemy of his symbol, Pindar will show that Hieron has indeed accompanied him as another manifestation of the same civilizing force that is Greek music or culture.

Pythia I

Hieron is a king —perhaps, as the poet believes or hopes, a great king. For him a victory in the games is but an ornament to an already wide renown. The actual victory, therefore, is cast by the poet, as apparently by Hieron himself, in a role secondary to the patron's greater achievements; for Hieron of Syracuse had had himself proclaimed at the Pythian course with the epithet "Aetnean," a word which until recently had signified a volcano, but now, through the king's colonization, would name a city. This act of founding a city, an outpost of the Greek civic ideal, on Aetna, plays the image of Hieron upon the hieratic pose of Zeus, the Conqueror of the Giants; and in this function, that of imposing celestial order upon the monsters in Chaos, Zeus appears, himself a poet, for it is music, the paeans of Pierides, that sounds the retreat for his enemies. The parallel between Zeus and Hieron is emphasized by structural balance, for Hieron is first introduced in this poem in an oblique development from the return to the theme of Zeus and his enemies, the theme which frames the cyclic digression on Typhos and Aetna.

The myth itself has a peculiarly exciting texture, since the recent eruption of Aetna provides visual proof, in the mythological language, of the horrific monster Zeus has chained beneath the very island of Sicily. The vividness of the description of the fires flowing from Typhos merges ancient with contemporary history:

> The mountain's core disgorges dread and holy streams of
> fire
> No touch profanes: rivers by day pour smoke
> In burning flow, but in night's
> Darkness, crimson flames
> Of rolling rock to ocean's
> Deep plain plunge, explode!

In the coalescence of myth and history we see the same immediacy that produced the *Persians* of Aeschylus. Myth was not some far-distant folktale language; it was remembered history, and the great events of the present are themselves new events in myth. The image of Aetna's colonization superimposed upon that of Typhos' subjugation has established the identity of Zeus and Hieron; this equation will be applied in the poem to extract the significance from other historical events. For Typhos, bound beneath the earth, is localized at Cumae, the vicinity of Vesuvius, as well as beneath the island of Sicily. The poet will apply the preconditioned Zeus-Hieron coincidence to his patron's victory over the Etruscans in this other place where the giant Typhos was manifest. By a volitional confusion, moreover, Hieron's victory over the Phoenicians at Himera is displaced and fused with the battle at Cumae. Hieron's actions in war, therefore, appear a mere refocusing of his earlier hieratic pose as conqueror of the volcano:

> ... today
> The Phoenician and the Etruscans' war-cry
> Will stay at home when they see their pride
> Weeping for the ships at Cumae
> And how they suffered, conquered by the lord of
>   Syracuse, who cast
> Their youth wide of the swift-cleaving
> Ships into the sea,
> Relieving Greece from slavery's burden. . . .

In delivering Greece from slavery, the war-lord reappears as civilizer: Hieron had defended the west while the Athenians and Spartans repelled the Persians in the east. The forces of barbarism on both fronts were dispersed. Once again triumphant over disorder have sounded the paeans of Pierides.

A passage earlier in the ode had indeed transubstantiated the human general, Hieron, to something almost divine, for he is a living example of the wounded hero whose magical powers will save mankind. The real Hieron, who suffered

from kidney stones, is, in the poet's double vision, like Philoctetes, who, despite the ulcerating sore on his foot, was
needed at Troy before that eastern city could fall to the army
of Greeks. There is connoted, therefore, something of necessity in Hieron's victories.

Hieron himself emerges more from the various ap-
proaches to definition than through any single aspect of his
whole significance. He is the power of the lyre; he is the great
colonizer, the conqueror of giants, the divinely blessed warrior. The future alone remains as an obstacle. To surpass even
this, there is need of the patron's son and the poet's control
of harmony.

Nothing in Pindar's odes is more subtle, more astounding,
than the intricate movement from the exact environmental
description of the banquet entertainment to what develops
into the complete apotheosis of music. The invocation to the
lyre has extended music's significance to that of a universal
principle; it remains for the rest of the ode to apply to the
poet's particular commission the beneficent influence of harmony. Invocation connotes prayer, and the formal require-
ment is satisfied only by the ensuing specific requests
addressed to the new god-like power. The prayer is three-
fold, addressed first with reference to Aetna, then Hieron, and
finally Deinomenes, the son of Hieron. And in each case, as is
the nature of prayer, the request looks forward to the journey
into the future.

Aetna's prayer is at once simple and complex. The city is
new, as yet without a heritage. The poet asks the lyre's god,
Apollo, to "make this land brave," to make it a place that will
continue to be a suitable theme for poets. The complexity involves the poet's masterful subordination of Hieron's Pythian
victory to the dominant theme of Aetna's future. Hieron, who
has won in Apollo's games, becomes merely a first instance of

Aetna's greatness; his victory is a favorable omen for the voyage toward the city's as yet unproven fame:

> Men who trust their lives to ships take
> Chief delight embarking with escorting
> Wind; it augurs well
> For safe return. These present victories have led
> Me to conclude a future city renowned in wreaths
> And horses, where music celebrates festivity.

Aetna's greatness requires the talent god channels into three classes of men: the poet, the warrior, and the statesman. That is to say, there is need for the arts of government and war and for the inspired words of a poet who will bear them true witness:

> For from you gods are born all means to mortal excellence:
>   the inspired,
> The strong of hand, the eloquent derive from you.

The truth of the witness is, however, vital. Through music's power, Pindar will attempt to strike a balance between pain and happiness, the aspiration to greatness and the frailty of our human condition. He sees himself about to hurl a bolt of melody; and, in a metaphor taken from the games, he seeks words for the critical equilibrium which will phrase a sufficient, although not falsely extravagant, claim for Hieron's prosperity:

> The bronze-tipped javelin
> Balanced in my hand I hope
> To cast not farther than the precinct
> Of the games, but merely to surpass my rivals' throw.

It is by such a meditation that Pindar modulates to the theme of Hieron and the prayer, or rather, prayers (for there are two), that he will address on his patron's behalf. Both look to time for their completion. The first asks simply that Hieron continue in his happiness and that from the vantage-point of his success he look with failing memory back upon the pain of his physical disease. In a sense, music and the careful control of themes have such therapeutic power. The second prayer is more ambitious. By imposing on Hieron the paradigm of Philoctetes, music can produce the expectation that Hieron too might escape his chronic illness:

Might there be for Hieron too a god who cures,
Judicious in apportioning success secure through time's approach!

The second prayer is really the first rephrased, and with the added burden of the Philoctetes exemplar.

A son is a man's continuator into the future if he is worthy of his father, if he is a legitimate heir. The poet readdresses the Muse and turns to his final subject, Deinomenes, who will be, by this ode, inaugurated as Aetna's king. His introduction is somewhat abrupt, no doubt because the epinician structure is being used here in a new fashion to fit the exigencies of a coronation anthem. Deinomenes, the poet says, has a right to his share of praise because he too is happy about his father's victory. The poet in his role as teacher recalls to Deinomenes' mind the Dorian constitution which Hieron has transferred from the Peloponnesus to Aetna. This passage on the nation's heritage culminates in the poet's third prayer; he asks that Deinomenes, true to the legalistic foundation of his city, play the role of musician and strike a concord between the peers of his dominion and his own tyrannical power:

O Zeus who bring fulfillment, award these people and
    their kings a destiny
No different here beside Amenas' water: forever
Valid subject of men's eulogy.
By your aid, the head of state
Would honor then and turn
The commons to harmonious peace hereditary.

Victory at Delphi has become, by the poet's melodic modulation, a hymn for coronation. The epinician necessity to eulogize is applied now to the as-yet-untried and unaccomplished king. In Pindar's most elaborate variation of the cliché that victory incurs a debt that the poet pays in panegyric, he recalls the battles of Salamis and Plataea and the obligations they imposed on him for song. Himera and Cumae are on a par with these, and they too demand reward. In a staccato series of gnomic statements, he meditates on the discords that threaten an improper payment. The passage is a doublet, in different terms, of the earlier javelin-metaphor he had applied to Hieron's eulogy. The poet must be succinct but must not fall short of the mark; he must praise fully, though full praise incites jealousy. Even so, the danger must be met; he will forge the truthful phrase:

Were you, my art, to measure praise in due proportion, and yet
    yet
Succinctly in a word compress it all, criticism would be less
Severe: satiety unending blunts
Keen expectation's edge;
Nothing so aggravates the hidden
Greed of citizens as hearing of possessions
Not their own. Howbeit —envy is preferred
To pity— neglect not excellence.
Steer your boat with justice: forge
A tongue on truth's anvil.

As the poem works back to the image of the banquet-hall and the resounding lyre, it becomes increasingly obvious that what Pindar is doing here is a most scrupulous demonstration of the poet's task of bringing into harmony the unformed elements for his composition. Deinomenes is being awarded a eulogy consistent with the expectation for his and Aetna's greatness, but one which does not falsify the fact that he must still prove himself. He is instructed by a medley of epinician clichés and political apothegms. If so he act, he need merely spread his sail to travel in the poet's ship on that favorable voyage toward Aetna's glory. The fame the poet will award will not be flattery but that truth which alone can stand the test of time. His praise, then, is a choice of paradigms. Hieron was Philoctetes; it is up to Deinomenes to be a Croesos and not a Phalaris:

> Men's boast of fame
> Transcending mortal life
> Is justified or not, and only this reveals, to future
> Poets and historians, the life they led:
> Croesos is remembered as beneficent,
> While hatred's prison holds the memory of cruel
> Phalaris, whose brazen bull burned men alive.
> Not him in banquet-hall do lyres receiving share
> With chanting boys.

This striving for excellence is the meaning of the contest at Delphi. The prize has changed from the wreath of laurel to a city's coronal and perhaps, if the ruler produces harmony, to an even more transcendent crown.

Paradoxically, the symbol of the lyre both unifies and destroys "Pythia I." The excitement it occasions charms us into neglecting the other parts of this poem. It is true the lyre radiates from its golden nucleus a synoptic series of particularized manifestations, emerging now as Zeus the Civilizer, now as Hieron, or the new king of Aetna; but the very incandescence of the beginning makes all returns to the theme but faint reflectors which play back the light and add slight luster of their own. The poem dims without a triumphant resurgence at its end. The cause, no doubt, is the difficulty of the commission, an epinician ode to celebrate not what the poet had seen at Delphi but the uncertainty of an unknown monarch's reign. The poem therefore seems more bravado than vision, more sheer virtuosity than inspiration. It is strange that Pindar's one true symbol did not produce his best poem. The poem can be analyzed most neatly; its structures can be elucidated. But the resonance of counterpoised parts here sounds not quite in key. It is the conflagration which destroys analysis that fires our minds; the music no instrument can play delights us most.

Pythia I: For Hieron of Aetna: Victory With Chariot

ΧΡΥΣΕΑ ΦΟΡΜΙΓΞ ΑΠΟΛΛΩΝΟΣ ΚΑΙ ΙΟΠΛΟΚΑΜΩΝ

STROPHE

Behold the gold, this lyre: you, Apollo's wealth in common
With the Muses (their hair inwoven violet): harkens
Dance, the source of festival, while
Poets yield to rhythms
You so finely flashing
Fashion, yours the step in prelude
To the chorus —you who quench the lightning's spear
Of ever-flowing fire: sleeps
The eagle, swift wings folded,
Upon the staff of Zeus,

ANTISTROPHE

His sovereign bird, and black the face of cloud, sweet
    prisoning
Of sight, your poured, enshrouding curve-beaked head:
His back, in slumber, ripples liquid,
Possessed by measured surge —

161

Violent Ares, his sharp
Spears' edge abandoned, here
Relents, entranced. Yours the arrows now
That stun the minds of gods:
Of Leto's son this art, and Muses
Robed in flowing folds.

EPODE

Whatever Zeus has never loved, in rout bewildered
Hears paeans of Pierides by land
And on unvanquished sea:
So lies in fearful Tartaros an enemy of gods,
Typhos hundred-headed: he it was who
Once was nourished in the famed Cilician cave; now
Chains, the sea-fenced heights of Cumae
And Sicilian land, oppress
His shaggy chest —heaven's pillar holds him,
Snow-swept Aetna, year-long
Nurse of jagged ice.

STROPHE

The mountain's core disgorges dread and holy streams of fire
No touch profanes: rivers by day pour smoke
In burning flow, but in night's
Darkness, crimson flames
Of rolling rock to ocean's
Deep plain plunge, explode!
That beast's the cause: from him gush up horrific
Well-springs of Hephaestos —a wondrous
Prodigy to see, a wonder too
For those who listen here:

ANTISTROPHE

Thus is he bound among the black-leaved peaks of Aetna
And on the plain; the bed, a goad whereon he lies, tears
Furrows down his back. May
Not I incur your wrath,

Pythia I

O Zeus, whose mountain, crown
Of this fertile land, gave honor to a city,
Near-by, founded in its name, and grew
In glory, triumphant at the Pythian course,
Proclaimed by herald announcing: "Victor
In the chariot race, Hieron

EPODE

Of Aetna": Men who trust their lives to ships take
Chief delight embarking with escorting
Wind; it augurs well
For safe return. These present victories have led
Me to conclude a future city renowned in wreaths
And horses, where music celebrates festivity.
Lycean lord and king of Delos, O
Phoebos Apollo, who love
The Castalian spring of Mount Parnassos, may you now
With favor hear my prayer: make
This land brave.

STROPHE

For from you gods are born all means to mortal excellence:
     the inspired,
The strong of hand, the eloquent derive from you. Zealous
As I am to praise this man,
The bronze-tipped javelin
Balanced in my hand I hope
To cast not farther than the precinct
Of the games, but merely to surpass my rivals' throw.
Might time throughout its course
Maintain him fortunate in grant of wealth,
Obliterate the memory of pain!

ANTISTROPHE

Time would summon then to his remembrance only that,
     courageous, he
Withstood both war and illness when such glory

At the hands of gods they found as no
Greek ever culled before,
The lordly crown on riches.
In present instance he, like Philoctetes,
Took the field: and all, however arrogant,
Fawned perforce and called him friend.
Heroes, it is said, the peers of gods,
Came once to Lemnos

EPODE

Seeking the weak and wounded archer, Poias' son:
With them he plundered Priam's town
And finished the Danaans' task.
His flesh was sick but in him walked divinity.
Might there be for Hieron too a god who cures,
Judicious in apportioning success secure through time's
     approach!
Deinomenes —my Muse, for him reward no less
With song the four-horse
Team: no alien joy his father's prize.
Come now, for Aetna's king
Elaborate his share of praise!

STROPHE

In his behalf this city with god-built freedom Hieron
Founded on the laws whose guide-lines Hyllos traced:
The race of Pamphylos and the sons of Heracles
Who dwell beneath Taygetos
Choose to stay forever
Dorian within the statutes of Aegimios.
They came from Pindos and settled rich in Amyclae,
High-honored neighbors of the white-
Horsed Tyndarids. And their fame
Of spear-point flowered.

ANTISTROPHE

O Zeus who bring fulfillment, award these people and their
     kings a destiny

Pythia I

No different here beside Amenas' water: forever
Valid subject of men's eulogy.
By your aid, the head of state
Would honor then and turn
The commons to harmonious peace hereditary.
Hear my supplication, son of Cronos: today
The Phoenician and the Etruscans' war-cry
Will stay at home when they see their pride
Weeping for the ships at Cumae

EPODE

And how they suffered, conquered by the lord of Syracuse,
    who cast
Their youth wide of the swift-cleaving
Ships into the sea,
Relieving Greece from slavery's burden: my wage
For singing Salamis, Athenian friendship; I sang in Sparta,
Too, for the battles beneath Cithaeron where Persians fell,
Archers of the curved bow; now the coast
At Himera, rich in water —
This victory earns a hymn wherein my duty is fulfilled,
The praise Deinomenids receive for valor
In beating back their enemy.

STROPHE

Were you, my art, to measure praise in due proportion,
    and yet
Succinctly in a word compress it all, criticism would be less
Severe: satiety unending blunts
Keen expectation's edge;
Nothing so aggravates the hidden
Greed of citizens as hearing of possessions
Not their own. Howbeit —envy is preferred
To pity— neglect not excellence.
Steer your boat with justice: forge
A tongue on truth's anvil.

ANTISTROPHE

The slightest fire kindled is called great when it comes
    from you,
Deinomenes: of many you are the steward; many witness
Evil or good and are believed.
Abiding in this flower of your nature,
To hear yourself fair-
Spoken, spare no expense;
And like a pilot unfurl your sail to catch
The wind. Be not deceived, my friend,
By fickle gain. Men's boast of fame
Transcending mortal life

EPODE

Is justified or not, and only this reveals, to future
Poets and historians, the life they led:
Croesos is remembered as beneficent,
While hatred's prison holds the memory of cruel
Phalaris, whose brazen bull burned men alive.
Not him in banquet-hall do lyres receiving share
With chanting boys. A good life wins
First prize; good
Reputation second; but whosoever chance on both of these
And grasp them firm, on him alone
Is placed the highest crown.

Pythia III: Manifesto and Consolatory

The sacred cantatas of Bach present a world whose diversity is the more exciting for its basic unity. This is, of course, a commonplace of baroque music, for always the imagination of both performer and composer is pitted against the coherence of sameness. Bach, however, excels his contemporaries in invention; the cantatas are not predictable —those of Telemann, for example, are— and each new wonder summons remembrance of so many masterful victories over the same material. Such is, obviously, also true of Pindar, for the odes have no universally applied technique. By a novel instrumentation, a daring balance, Bach almost persuades us that some tenet of religion is an original discovery; Pindar's "meditations," despite their, for the most part, predetermined and culturally ordained conclusions, strike the tone of valid hard thought. Assuredly, the ode grants immortality of a kind; Pindar's statement, however, which —by so nearly eluding our comprehension in its intricacy— casts a darkness, reemerges triumphant with the new conviction lighting what we already know.

The occasion for "Pythia III" determines its, as it were, minor key. The illness, perhaps the approaching death, of

Hieron deflects the ode's order of events; the distant memory
of glory at Pytho should, but apparently does not, compensate for the reality of human mortality. Traditional consolation is, as Valéry has said, a pious ruse: *"Maigre immortalité
noire et dorée,/ Consolatrice affreusement laurée."* It is thus
that Pindar preludes his attenuated rehearsal of the commonplace by the entire ode, which has the form of a wish, a
prayer addressed to no divinity, since no divinity is apposite;
indeed, the burden of the myth is to work back to a doublet-
rephrasing of the wish, which will show in starker lines that
by nature it is contrary to fulfillment. Only with the second
statement of the wish are we told for whom the poem is
written and why the poet has made the wish.

The poet had begun with his own expression of a wish
he says the patron's populace also shares—the simple desire
that the dead Chiron were still alive. The poignancy of the
wish is emphasized, for it is interrupted before proceeding
to its elaboration, by the poet's notice of his own impotency
in this regard; Chiron is, of course, gone. Instead of the
reason for the wish, we are presented with what at first
appears to be but an additional ornament to the name of
Chiron: it was that Centaur who had taught Asclepios the
art of medicine. And again by apparent misdirection, the
poet digresses to the story of Asclepios' birth, an unnatural
birth, since his mother, Coronis, had angered Apollo and had
died by the arrows of Artemis, a metaphor for the pain of
childbirth. Instead of his birth, then, we have recorded the
apparent negation of his birth, a paradox which will be
solved only later in the poem. The poem thus is raising more
questions than it answers. Through a technique that Pindar
uses repeatedly in this ode, the segment of narration concludes in an apothegm:

> Thus not to no effect the children
> Of Zeus are angered!

The referent is immediate and in a sense also yet to come,
for the homily comments on Apollo's anger, and at the same

time establishes the subject for the next segment of narration; moreover, it maintains, by its gnomic style, a certain autonomy which will allow it to remain in suspension until the final gathering for the ode's teaching.

We proceed backward, then, to the cause of Apollo's anger: he had slept with Coronis and got her with child; she jeopardized her pregnancy, however, by an elopement with another man. The point of this segment is reached in an application of the woman's failing broadened to all mankind:

> . . . . she loved
> What she did not have —a common failing.
> There is a strain of men most foolish
> That scorns the near because it sees the far,
> Tracking down illusions and fruitless hopes.

It is interesting that the narrative is almost flattened to what amounts to two concomitant events, the quasi-adultery of Coronis and her death; for instead of receding to an anterior event, the same segment of narration is repeated with additional coloration: Coronis sleeps with the stranger from Arcadia, and Apollo, in his omniscience —a new attribute of divinity— learns all and ordains her death. Her death, however, now appears more Apollo's act than his sister's, for it is perhaps a plague that kills her and many of her neighbors. The wider focus of suffering assumes the Hesiodic basis for sin and retribution, in which a whole people pay with corporate guilt for the error of one in their midst. There is, however, something subliminally right in this statement of wider suffering, which answers the broadened application of Coronis' failing in the preceding gnomic passage; it is as though they all shared Coronis' dissatisfaction with what was at hand. The section concludes in an apothegm which parallels the preceding conclusion: a sin had been generalized; retribution now receives the same treatment:

> . . . . the fire
> Leaps on a mountain,
> From a single spark obliterating all the forest.

Curiously, the transition to the next segment of narration, a repetition of Asclepios' birth which this time solves the earlier paradox, is effected by the same technique as before —a gnomic summary which states as well the new theme— only this time the theme is stated almost by pure word-association: fire induces fire, and we are shown the funeral pyre of Coronis. A well-phrased traditional thought has, for Pindar, the same function as a poetic image. It is indeed this equivalence which makes a Pindaric ode a meditation rather than a preaching, since thought is manipulated by procedures germane to poetry, and poetry is indistinguishable from the processes of thought. The excitement of so novel a thought-process makes the actual teaching of the poem irrelevant for us; we need not pause to question whether or not we agree, for such would be like asking ourselves if we "agreed" with a melody in music. To choose at random an opposite example, we need merely think of the bald preaching of a poem by Victor Hugo. We are embarrassed by his thought but latch onto it, there being little else in the poem. . . .

Although engendered by word-association, the narrative apparently develops toward a paradigmatic teaching of its own; later it will prove to be contributory to the total meaning. Apollo had, at the last moment, taken pity on his unborn son and wrenched him from his dead mother's womb. Asclepios, therefore, in his birth, presents an anticipatory illustration that a man can be resurrected from the dead. His use as an exemplar of this idea achieves greater clarity as Pindar proceeds to amplify his earlier mention that Asclepios was taught by Chiron the art of medicine:

And his patients who came, some their flesh
A mere companion possessed by sores,
Or limbs by grey bronze
Wounded or by far-flung
Stone; others the body ravaged by fever's summer

Heat or winter chill —each he delivered from his
    separate pain:
Ministering to some with gentle incantation or
    palliatives
To drink; or applying ointments which he gathered;
With surgeon's knife
Still others he made to stand upright.

The paradigm turns around, however. Not only was Asclepios
himself saved from death, but he, for a princely wage, agreed
to employ his art to perform a Lazarus-like miracle and bring
a corpse back to life. At the moment when he seems most to
exemplify the hope of resurrection, he is destroyed by the
thunderbolt of Zeus for having attempted what must not be
done. The conclusion is again gnomic, an eloquent passage
which has inspired Valéry's *Cimetière Marin* and Camus'
Mythe de Sisyphe:

We must from our mortality ask gods
Our duty and our rights,
Knowing what lies before us, man's condition.
Do not, my soul, essay the life immortal
But exhaust the reservoir of what your art can do.

It is at this point that we realize the significance of Pindar's
use of the word for art or poetry to designate the profession
of Asclepios:

But even his art was a slave: he had his price.
Gold in the buyer's hand subverted
Even him.

Such a statement in a Pindaric poem usually refers to the
difficult situation the poet faces in attempting to balance
truthful expression and the patron's possible inducements
for more extravagant glory. Its application here to Asclepios
makes him stand as a warning to Pindar of the extreme
danger he would encounter were he to promise more than
poetry can do. Certainly poetry grants an immortality of a

kind, but here it is a question of continuance in real existence.
The poet cannot attempt so hazardous a task.

What, then, can he do? At this moment of complete reversal in the poem, when optimism has been dashed to the
opposite tones, the introductory wish is restated. It is this
that the poet had had in his mind, and the restatement bears
the full melancholy of the realization that he had been yearning for what could not be. If Chiron were still alive, then
Pindar, by his songs, would have charmed him to teach another doctor who might save men from disease and death;
and Pindar would have gone to Syracuse to cure his friend.
The celebration for a Pythian victory —some vaguely referred to, imprecise event— would have been converted into
the personification of health, who would step off the ship:

Yes, if Chiron still were dwelling sagacious in his cave,
And if some charm there were the music of my song might
    lay
Upon his heart, why then I would persuade him
To provide a doctor for the fevers of good men —
Someone sprung from Leto, some Apollo.
And I would sail cutting the Ionian sea
To Arethousa's spring and the court of my Aetnean host,
. . . .
To him a double joy —
Were I to disembark and bring golden health and
    celebration
For the Pythian games, wreathed radiance that in his
    finest moment Pherenicos
Won that time at Cirrha— I mean a light
More brilliant than heaven's star
Would I arrive
After my voyage across the deep sea.

The passage is the more moving in that it recalls so many
other poetic journeys the poet had made, embarked in this

cliché. The light that will not come becomes a darkness; and the celebration, deprived of its essential concomitant for the ailing Hieron, becomes a weak affair, a radiance dimmed by the years that have passed since the horse Pherenicos ran. What was implied earlier in the double vision of poet as doctor now determines the indecisive naming of the doctor Chiron would have taught; for it would have been the poet himself, perhaps, who would have played that role, had he gone to the court of Hieron. The tension of the contrary-to-fact condition has perhaps never been so strong.

The vanity of all that has preceded in this ode is felt; and the poet puts away from himself the magnificent conceit that had come to him. He will present a consolation, an unassuming substitution for what he must not do. And if we may believe the ancient accounts of Pindar's encounter with revealed religion, we know how sincere this substitution is. While traveling on a mountain in a storm, Pindar had that hallucinatory experience common to travelers in lonely places. In Pindar's version of the phenomenon, he saw a statue of the Great Mother fall at his feet; and in consequence of this vision, he dedicated a shrine near his home to her and Pan. It is to these gods who grant communion and perhaps salvation to man that Pindar says he will pray. The prayer is not stated, but it can no doubt be read from the poet's refusal to essay immortal life: he will pray for what his poetry dare not do.

The poet has disillusioned himself; he must now persuade his patron to accept his mortal condition. Pindar presents Hieron an exegesis on the sacred text of Homer. Zeus, in the *Iliad*, has at his door two jars, one filled with good things, and the other with bad; in the parable he dips twice into the jar of bad things for each dip into the good, and thus he makes his dispensations to man. That is the reality of our existence, and we must find some way to bear nobly the adversity that is our lot. Nobility consists in presenting a façade to the world, of hiding one's troubles and showing only happiness:

> Moreover, Hieron, if you comprehend the basic meaning
> Of a story, you know then what the ancient poet taught:
> For every good, two evils the immortals
> Grant. This dispensation the mature alone,
> Unlike the base,
> Can bear with poise, displaying only good.

It is true that Hieron has an inordinate grant of good, for he is a king and has the paramountcy of prosperity. But he must expect reversal; indeed his sickness is an example of what, in the order of things, must be. Two mythological paradigms —Cadmos and Peleus— are compared to Hieron in their happiness, but even they met reversal. It is the nature of change, however, to continue changing. Cadmos was compensated for the loss of his three daughters by the fact that one of them conceived by Zeus the god Dionysos; and Peleus, who lost his son Achilles in the war at Troy, perhaps found solace in the fact that the entire army wept for his loss. Hieron, too, it is implied, will have his compensation; for he is most surely, in his abundance and his suffering, like the paradigms. It is indeed for such a new change that the poet apparently will pray.

Philosophical thought through the language of mythological exemplars sometimes misleads, since it may strike harmonic reverberations which, although pleasing for what they add to total poetic coherence, partially obstruct comprehension. Thus, the funeral pyre of Achilles recalls Coronis' death; Semele's union with Zeus recalls that of Apollo with Coronis; and the vestals who sing songs at Pindar's door recall the hymeneal hymns not sung for Coronis. It is a phenomenon similar to that which we noticed in the word-association transition on "fire." The story of Coronis has established certain modes of expression in the poet's mind, and these find reexpression in transmuted form as the poet goes on to speak of other things.

So, too, the narrative segments of Peleus and Cadmos conclude, as did the fragmented story of Coronis, with an apothegmatic statement:

> But the mortal who within
> His own mind knows the path of truth will surely find
> Happiness amongst the Blessed. Variable the gusts
> Of high hovering winds: prosperity
> Goes not far
> Secure, when followed by the burden of its abundance.

The statement summarizes the final happiness that Peleus and Cadmos found, despite their fall. It introduces as well the final subject of the poem, the problem which had been latent throughout the ode—the manner the poet should use in eulogy. He had denied himself the highest hope, only to reappraise, through the substitution of a prayer, and paradigms of an upward change that followed upon a downward one, the possibility of that high hope, somewhat tempered now by humility. His eulogy will match his subject, variable in the same degree as is his station:

> Humble in a humble state and great in greatness,
> We fashion with our wits the fortune that befalls us,
> Doctoring it according to our art.

This is our duty and our right. We cannot escape reversal; we cannot escape death. The poet cannot bring physical continuance, but, in the manner of a choral, he rediscovers the old truth that poetry grants some permanence to supremacy. Nestor and Sarpedon are posed as examples that a man's fame, if it has become a poet's theme, lives after him. Pindar assumes the role of doctor, and applies to poets the designation he had at the beginning of the ode used for Asclepios. The speed of the conclusion is dazzling and the abrupt transitions almost escape our comprehension. We are aware only that, after all, there is some consolation in poetry; the poet will do, at least in part, what we thought he could not do — although we had always thought, before this ode, that that *was* what poetry did. The burden of the meditation, however, has made this basic tenet of the eulogistic ode seem somehow profound; and it is upon this sensed profundity that the poet builds his declaration of the difficulty inherent in his task.

PYTHIA III: For Hieron of Syracuse:
On the Occasion of His Illness

ΗΘΕΛΟΝ ΧΙΡΩΝΑ ΚΕ ΦΙΛΤΡΙΔΑΝ

STROPHE

If only Chiron, Philyra's child
(Granted it be right my tongue should voice
This prayer that many share)
Were living —but he is gone,
The son of Cronos and the line of Ouranos: wide was his
    dominion —
If only still he ruled the woods of Pelion; though beast and
    wild,
His mind was tame: for so he taught
That artisan of cures and strengthened limbs,
Gentle Asclepios
The magnificent who delivered men from all disease.

ANTISTROPHE

His mother, noble Phlegyas' daughter,
Never bore him with Eleithyia's aid
But succumbed before her time
To the golden arrows of Artemis

And went down to the house of Hades from her bridal
    chamber:
Apollo plotted her death. Thus not to no effect the children
Of Zeus are angered! She had slighted him —stupid sin!—
And chose another marriage her father
Did not sanction:
Already she had lain with Phoebos, his hair of youth

EPODE

Unshorn, and even then was carrying the god's immaculate
    seed.
She had no patience to await the wedding-feast
Nor her attendants' jubilant nuptial-cry, suggestive
Rite young girls, naive companions of her age,
At evening sing. Not at all: she loved
What she did not have —a common failing.
There is a strain of men most foolish
That scorns the near because it sees the far,
Tracking down illusions and fruitless hopes.

STROPHE

Ah yes, this fatal tendency bewildered
The mind of rich-robed Coronis:
When the stranger came from Arcadia,
She shared her bed with him.
But this went not unnoticed: Pytho's lord
Loxias sat in his temple recipient of sacrifice and knew all,
Convinced by immediate proof, his own omniscience,
Witness that falsehood cannot touch,
That nothing deceives,
Not god nor mortal, neither act nor thought.

ANTISTROPHE

He apprehended in a moment the lawless guile:
Ischys, the guest, Eilatos' son,
Welcomed to her bed; and sent
His sister raging, inspired,

178

Pythia III

Irresistible, to Lacereia where the girl lived near the cliffs that
  border
Lake Boebias. Fortune took a turn for the worse and struck her
  down —
But not alone, for many was the neighbor who shared
Her fate, dying in the holocaust: the fire
Leaps on a mountain,
From a single spark obliterating all the forest.

EPODE

But when within a wall of wood her kinsmen placed
The girl, and the ravenous blaze Hephaestos ran
Encircling, then only did Apollo speak: "Enough!
What I have sown, my conscience cannot bring to nothing;
I pity my child's death compassed in its mother's."
Those were his words. With one step he was there
And snatched the infant from the corpse; the burning
Pyre parted. He brought him to the Magnesian Centaur
To learn the cures for painful human sicknesses.

STROPHE

And his patients who came, some their flesh
A mere companion possessed by sores,
Or limbs by grey bronze
Wounded or by far-flung
Stone; others the body ravaged by fever's summer
Heat or winter chill —each he delivered from his separate
  pain:
Ministering to some with gentle incantation or palliatives
To drink; or applying ointments which he gathered;
With surgeon's knife
Still others he made to stand upright.

ANTISTROPHE

But even his art was a slave: he had his price.
Gold in the buyer's hand subverted
Even him; for a princely wage

He escorted back from the dead
A man already taken. Therefore the hand of Cronion
Cast transfixing both and took from their lungs life's breath
In an instant; the fiery thunderbolt dashed death.
We must from our mortality ask gods
Our duty and our rights,
Knowing what lies before us, man's condition.

EPODE

Do not, my soul, essay the life immortal
But exhaust the reservoir of what your art can do.
Yes, if Chiron still were dwelling sagacious in his cave,
And if some charm there were the music of my song might lay
Upon his heart, why then I would persuade him
To provide a doctor for the fevers of good men —
Someone sprung from Leto, some Apollo.
And I would sail cutting the Ionian sea
To Arethousa's spring and the court of my Aetnean host,

STROPHE

Who in Syracuse is governor and king,
Benevolent to the citizens, not envying his nobles,
And to guests an admirable father.
To him a double joy —
Were I to disembark and bring golden health and celebration
For the Pythian games, wreathed radiance that in his
        finest moment Pherenicos
Won that time at Cirrha —I mean, a light
More brilliant than heaven's star
Would I arrive
After my voyage across the deep sea.

ANTISTROPHE

That cannot be. But I will pray
To our holy Mother who receives with Pan
The nightly homage vestals
In the temple sing by my door.

Moreover, Hieron, if you comprehend the basic meaning
Of a story, you know then what the ancient poet taught:
For every good, two evils the immortals
Grant. This dispensation the mature alone,
Unlike the base,
Can bear with poise, displaying only good.

EPODE

Your role entails good fortune: on the tyrant
Who leads the people —if on any man—
There looks the greatest destiny. But life without reversal
Neither Peleus, Aeacos' son, nor that peer of gods,
Cadmos, ever had: each, of mortals, possessed
The summit of prosperity and heard on the mountain or at
    Thebes
Seven-gated, the Muses dancing, their hair
Gold-bound, when one wed *mélancolique* Harmonia,
And the other wise Nereus' daughter, Thetis.

STROPHE

No less than gods banqueted with them
And each saw the children of Cronos,
Kings on golden thrones,
And received their marriage-gifts,
Through the grace of Zeus, exchanging previous troubles for
    a heart
Uplifted. But yet, in time, three daughters suffered sharp
Pain and bereft the one of his share in happiness:
This notwithstanding, Zeus the Father
Came to Thyona,
Her white arms and the bed for which he lusted.

ANTISTROPHE

The other's son, the only child
Immortal Thetis bore in Phthia,
In war —an arrow— abandoned
Life, and burning on the pyre,

181

Aroused the Danaans to lament. But the mortal who within
His own mind knows the path of truth will surely find
Happiness amongst the Blessed. Variable the gusts
Of high hovering winds: prosperity
Goes not far
Secure, when followed by the burden of its abundance.

EPODE

Humble in a humble state and great in greatness,
We fashion with our wits the fortune that befalls us,
Doctoring it according to our art. If god should grant us
    luxury
Of wealth, we have the hope of finding lofty fame
Hereafter. Nestor and Lycian Sarpedon are celebrities —
We know of them from rushing verses inspired
Builders, artisans, composed: excellence
Comes to be long-lived through song
Illustrious: for few is this an easy task.

Nemea III: "A Colossal Smile Off Him"

Once an art form has developed a life of its own, its own style and mannerisms, it becomes fair game for parody. And yet so august may be the original form that we are ashamed to entertain the possibility of a humorous statement. In such a circumstance, humor has a particularly ponderous tonality, like the pirouetting of a Klondike bear. The antics, moreover, are not mere interludes, but part of the work's total communication, as Claudel, who in our own time exemplified this quality of comedy, has said: "Ecoutez bien, ne toussez pas et essayez de comprendre un peu. C'est ce que vous ne comprendrez pas qui est le plus beau, c'est ce qui est le plus long qui est le plus intéressant et c'est ce que vous ne trouvez pas amusant qui est le plus drôle."

Thus when Pindar, in the poem he wrote for the Nemean victory of Aristocleides of Aegina, mocks himself, it is no wonder that the joke was glossed and missed by generations of serious-minded scholars.

> I send white milk with honey
> Mixed —foam brims the rim— elixir
> Singing in the flutes' Aeolic breath—

At long last. The eagle is a swift bird
To swoop upon the prey he circled from afar
Now bloodied in his talons.
Screaming blackbirds fly the lower air.

The biographical approach to poetry demanded that some
piece of history, personal or national, be found to give the
poem *some* meaning, however slight. Thus the blackbirds
either are or are not Bacchylides and his uncle Simonides,
and Pindar's poem, on the evidence of his own testimony, is
like a belated birthday card. The two references do not produce a coherent statement —that is to say, they have no context— but the uninspired have always assumed that such
confusions are the signs of inspiration.

The cliché in itself, the theme within a developed tradition, has lost the greater part of its interest for the poet and
his audience, except, of course, that its presence in the finished work produces the basic experience of security and
familiarity. This secure ground, as it were, allows the poet to
hazard extravagant flights of virtuosity. How far he impro-
vises upon this ground is a measure of his mastery. The audience is enticed by the danger of complete incomprehension,
although they never feel left out, since all that is there is
what, in another form, they have already known. As the poet
searches for wilder and wilder fantasies, he sometimes realizes the incongruity of it all, that he should stray so far from
the simple statement. He mocks his own situation and thereby
produces a still wilder fantasy.

The cliché of the poetic voyage once had some basis in
reality, for the poet was itinerant, and the ship that bore him
carried as well the festivity that his arrival would occasion.
If sometimes he did not go himself, the poem easily became
the cargo on board the ship. To write a poem therefore can
mean to take a voyage, a long voyage or a short one, depend-
ing on which route the poet chooses. Such then are some of
the simple variations that we see in other of Pindar's poems.

In "Nemea III" Pindar constructs a still more extreme variation. His ship is off its course; he has gone too far afield.

He had begun with an invocation summoning his Muse to take a journey to the island of Aegina, where a chorus is waiting to welcome her. There is a need for song, a thirst occasioned by the victor's triumph; it is the poet's task to supply the liqueur specific for this thirst, the milk with honey mixed, which at the end of the poem he, like a merchant, has apparently consigned to the shipment for Aegina. This outer variation induces a related elaboration. The *aristeia* of poetic composition is the concomitant, if not the metaphysical equivalent, for Pindar, of the athlete's achievement. By inversion thus, the victor has himself completed a voyage: his heredity from the ancient Myrmidons has "forged him to the rigors of the Voyage Pancration." He is, moreover, handsome; the beauty of his action is mirrored by his physical beauty. He is thus the true noble, the legitimate reincarnation of the ancient aristocratic ideal; he has reached the ultimate:

> . . . . he boards the zenith,
> This son of Aristophanes— how farther sail
> The unmapped sea beyond Gibraltar, ...

The mention of Gibraltar or the Pillars of Heracles is broached as an ornamental extension of the idea that the victor has made the ultimate journey. The metaphor, however, now deserts the victor and receives, in the typical archaic manner, independent treatment, as the poet launches into the mythical narrative of Heracles' journey to Gibraltar. The subject of Heracles, who performed so many labors, is not inapposite to the eulogy of a pancratiast, but Pindar does not develop the comparison. Instead, the theme is rejected; the poet has himself suddenly sailed off with Heracles and must now redirect his course:

> —my mind,
> Toward what exotic headland do you stray

> Our ship? Bring back the Muse to Aeacos's
> Dynasty.

After all, as he himself incongruously notes, the eulogistic
ode *does* have its rules:

> Most right the dictum: "Eulogize!"—
> Nor from abroad is satisfied what champions love.
> Look homeward! Here is your theme
> To sound some harmony.

He now most soberly chooses a theme that pertains more
nearly to the noble families of Aegina and he recounts in summary form the exploits of various Aeginetan epic heroes.
As if he wished to signal his awareness of the correct procedure, he even omits the name of Heracles from the mention
of the attack on Laomedon's Troy.

The narrative is complete; and, in what appears to be a
return to Aristocleides, Pindar contrasts the aristocrat with
his obverse, a hypothetical "new" man who can claim no
heritage of glory:

> Triumph is heredity's rich cargo. The parvenu
> In glory is a dull man,
> A feather in the wind; he disembarks, stumbles
> Off the ship a dilettante, who solely samples myriad merits.

We note, of course, that the parvenu's journey was a dismal
failure.

But again the poet's mind flies wild: our expectation is
defeated and the poem's completion is delayed, as he recalls how unlike the upstart was Achilles. A digression ensues
that narrates the education of Achilles and the other pupils in
Chiron's cave, Jason and Asclepios. His account touches on
the marriage of Peleus and Thetis, an item in the earlier
mythic section, and hastens on to Achilles' journey to Troy,
where he slew Memnon and kept *him* from his journey home.
Achilles thus emerges, by mistake and redirection, as the
theme proper, thereby realizing the implication in the earlier
mention of Aegina as the land where the "ancient Myrmidons

once dwelt." It is from him in particular that the island has its fame: "Whence arises rayonnant the Aeacid sun."

In true good order now, Pindar begins to treat again the material of the opening section. An eloquent statement that the test reveals the ultimate excellence in various categories —boy, man, and elder— is apparently a variation on the theme of Aristocleides, who has sailed the ultimate journey to the Pillars of Heracles, and who, by that very fact, belongs to a fourth category, something beyond the normal categories of human life. This fourth excellence defies labeling, unless of course it be called Aristocleides, to whom the poet modulates by abruptly substituting for the fourth class the dictum of his poetic genre, namely that he should praise the present victor. A centrifugal movement toward generalities is brought suddenly to earth, as the poet pounces on his particular theme (we might paraphrase: There are three classes of excellence, 1, 2, and 3; there is also a fourth, D . . . , a rule of my genre . . . which turns out to be you):

> But still a fourth to excellence
> Is wrought in mortal life . . . which tells us
> Mind the here-and-now —and that is you! Farewell,
> Friend.

The drink has come at last; the delay was occasioned not by any lapse in time between the victory and the poem, but only by the poet's pastiche of himself. He is the great eagle, the bird of birds, and perhaps the true fourth class, who hovers before he swoops on his prey, a transmutation which Pindar with full nobility has used elsewhere of himself. Here, however, it is perhaps parody, for the prey is his theme, Aristocleides. There is certainly something incongruous in its bloodied state, mauled in the talons of the great eagle; there is, however, no humility in this colossal smile, for the blackbirds, those lesser creatures, do scream, and the grace with which Aristocleides has been praised is worthy of the lyric grandeur that is Pindar's. Only a consummate style can be parodied —particularly by oneself.

NEMEA III: For Aristocleides of Aegina, Pancratiast

Ω ΠΟΤΝΙΑ ΜΟΙΣΑ ΜΑΤΕΡ ΑΜΕΤΕΡΑ ΛΙΣΣΟΜΑΙ

STROPHE

Lady, O Muse our mother, hear: this holy
Month Nemea come the welcome
Traveler to the Doric island of Aegina. By the waters
Of Asopos —come— they wait who build
Mellifluent festivity, young men who quest your voice.
Exploits each have thirsts unique:
But victory most our singing loves,
At hand to squire supremacy and wreaths.

ANTISTROPHE

Grant none cavil at my mind's choice words.
Begin, daughter to the Lord of Cloud
And Heavens, this hymn in eulogy: My task, the choral
Voice, the lyre's accompaniment: to grace
This land's delight, where ancient Myrmidons once
Dwelt. Their fabled forum not
With shame has Aristocleides stained —you
It was who forged him to the rigors of the Voyage

188

Nemea III

Pancration. Though bruised, exhausted, his cure
Restorative the "Hail, the victor!" brought
In Nemea's valley plain.
But he is handsome, too; his deeds mirror body's
Beauty: he boards the zenith,
This son of Aristophanes —how farther sail
The unmapped sea beyond Gibraltar, the Pillars Heracles,

STROPHE

The god and hero, placed, the frontier claim
His expedition staked. He tamed the ocean's
Monster beasts; he tracked, for curiosity, the currents
Of shoals to where he touched the point
That turned him home; he charted Earth —my mind,
Toward what exotic headland do you stray
Our ship? Bring back the Muse to Aeacos's
Dynasty. Most right the dictum: "Eulogize!" —

ANTISTROPHE

Nor from abroad is satisfied what champions love.
Look homeward! Here is your theme
To sound some harmony. The epics reveled in Peleus
The King: "Who cut a spear uncommon";
Who took Iolcos all alone without an army;
Laid violent hold of Thetis
Of the Sea. And brawny Telamon and Iolaos,
Comrades-in-arms, sacked Laomedon's Troy;

EPODE

Campaigned together, sought the Amazons'
Bronze archery; nor blunted quelling
Fear the edge of courage.
Triumph is heredity's rich cargo. The parvenu
In glory is a dull man,
A feather in the wind; he disembarks, stumbles
Off the ship a dilettante, who solely samples myriad merits.

STROPHE

But not red-blond Achilles: he began in Philyra's
House, a child who played the hero
(A toy, but fast as wind, the javelin hurled
To slaughter in the hunt wild lions
Or butcher boars; their carcasses he brought still throbbing
Home to Centaur Cronides . . . and that
When he was only six!) to become a hero
In his adulthood, awing Artemis and bold

ANTISTROPHE

Athena, for the deer that houndless, without traps, he
    killed —
So swift he ran! This tale, too,
The epics tell: how Chiron the Sage raised
Jason in his rock-roofed cave; later
Taught Asclepios his métier of balm and medicine;
And gave the bride away, Nereus' daughter,
Whose fruit was blessèd; nursled her son
Sublime, magnified his martial soul,

EPODE

That, sent on the wind-struck sea
To Troy's spear-clash, he stand the Lycian
"Alalai!," the Phrygian, and Dardanian;
He join in battle hand-to-hand with swordsmen Ethiops,
His idée fixe to see
Their chieftain not return back
Home, Helenos' wild and raging cousin, Memnon —

STROPHE

Whence arises rayonnant the Aeacid sun.
Zeus, yours their blood, this contest
Hymn-struck, choired by youth to cascade a land's
Delight. Our "Hail!" befits Aristocleides
Victor, who adds this island to his fame
And to his glory the sacred Pythian's confrerie.

Nemea III

The test distinguishes whatever be
Each category's consummate ideal:

ANTISTROPHE

For youth, the Boy of boys; the Man of men;
And third, the Elder —these the classes
Of our human race. But still a fourth to excellence
Is wrought in mortal life . . . which tells us
Mind the here-and-now —and that is you! Farewell,
Friend. I send white milk with honey
Mixed —foam brims the rim— elixir
Singing in the flutes' Aeolic breath—

EPODE

At long last. The eagle is a swift bird
To swoop upon the prey he circled from afar
Now bloodied in his talons.
Screaming black birds fly the lower air.
On you, as the throne of Clio
Willed, in that your stamina has borne
The prize, for Nemea, Epidauros, for Megara, the light has
shone.

NEMEA VII: The Alchemy of Silence

The succession of the dissenting disciples of Homer will culminate for Greek literature in Plato. His attempt to free thought from not only the accouterments of poetry but from its very basis marks a change in the Western tradition from poetic to prosaic modes of thinking. Plato's own success in exiling poetry from his republic but not from his mind testifies to the monumental will this transition required. Socrates before him had tried to stop the music by his dialectic, and in his interlocutor's sense of meaningless void as the truth of poetry vanished when submitted to examination and paraphrase, we have the first cause of that fear that was to lead to the death of Socrates. Earlier dissent was less radical. A Heraclitos, for example, might grumble that Homer should be tossed out of the rhapsodic contests, presumably because the truth of poetry was at variance with his own philosophy; but when he himself came to state the truth, his prose was to sound far more like poetry than physics. And the public's incomprehension must have made him feel, no doubt, like Ives, who said that his ears were on backwards, which is, of course, false naïveté implying that there is something wrong with us, not him.

And yet one did have to throw Homer out of the contests. It would be only after the growing dissent had achieved its purpose that we could stand outside the communication of poetry and judge it aesthetically. We have lost something, no doubt; poetry is not truth and we have learned not to care. The contemporary of Pindar did not have this freedom. Poetry for him was philosophy, or, indeed, philosophy was poetry. He had learned to reverence the Homer he had memorized. It was, however, increasingly more difficult to recognize or accept the truth masked in these poems: without a sense of relative historicity, he could not dismiss as anachronistic the bits of ethical wisdom that had been codified as the tradition. Nor did Homer and the subjects of his poems satisfy man's new areas of inquiry. Progress, however, of necessity moved in the old channels. No one writer could himself evolve a language suited to the potential of written, as against oral, communication; and if he had, no one could have understood him, for there was as yet no audience accustomed to reading rather than recalling. What we mean is this. Suppose our language were the rhythmic cadences and clichés of juke-box music. Our education would consist in our learning to manipulate this language, first merely to recall the words and melodies, then, if we are intelligent, to play our own variations upon the learned clichés. Suppose we wish, however, like Einstein, to investigate some problem about the organization of the cosmos. The task would not be impossible but the results would leave something to be desired. Rather than $E = mc^2$, we might well describe a lover's quarrel or a lament over waning virility. We have in the course of centuries escaped the confines of mythopoeic thought, and have indeed even come to recognize in the plurality of contemporary scientific jargons the probability that none of them alone catches the diversity there outside us. The ruler measures only in terms of its calibration. It is here, we might add, that we rediscover the truth of poetry; for in our recognition of the plurality of media, we wonder if perhaps the earliest has not still a right to deserve our serious consideration, especially since we did not as children know that we were to be rational, and since, consequently, the motives of our mature actions are basically mythopoeic.

There are difficulties, if we may anticipate objections, in our attempt to identify poetry as a mode of thought. It should be quite clear that once a new language has evolved —quantum physics, for example— a thought may occur in the new language and then be translated into poetry. We might, for example, recognize in a symbol the transfer of a rational concept into the clothing of poetry, whereas an image may be the same kind of idea which has occurred wholly within the poetic syntax. It is for this reason that it seems a fair question to ask of a symbol what it is it symbolizes. When we get the answer, we uncover that element in the rational syntax which was its origin. The same question cannot easily be answered for an image, since the answer requires all the inventiveness of an original translation. That is to say, we wish to define poetry here as mythopoeic logic and mnemonically-oriented phraseology. As such, it corresponds very well to the juke-box of our analogy. It also corresponds to the language of Pindar, although not so well —not so well because the dissenters from Homer, in whose company we shall place Pindar, use of necessity the juke-box language but strive for the solution of Einstein. The thought and the expression are poetic; the intent is "scientific."

Pindar's objection, as voiced in "Nemea VII," is complex. A simple objection would merely correct a predecessor's version of a myth. Such correction can achieve considerable subtlety, as, for example, in Xenophanes' description of deity, which is achieved by negating the narrative actions of Hesiod's Zeus. Or in Pindar himself, when in "Olympia VII" he revises history by shifting the emphasis in the events recorded in Homer's entry for Rhodes in the Catalogue of Ships. "Nemea VII," however, expresses a profound discontent with the poetic mode of communication —and this discontent is of course paradoxical, since Pindar is himself writing a poem. There are two things wrong with the poetic phenomenon: the poet's language and his audience's reception of it. Pindar cites two examples. Homer, by the beauty of his poem, has exaggerated the greatness of Odysseus:

> For in his fictions and contrivèd soar there is
> An awesome something: Poetry is thief,
> Through myth seductress of our minds.

When viewed this way, Homer is like Pindar's rival contemporaries, who employ the diapason of tinkling lies to overplay their patrons' eulogy. In other poems, this thought induces Pindar to reflect that such eulogy is vain and will not last. In "Nemea VII," however, the total vanity of human endeavor is the darker foil against which the poet must place his praise:

> Rich man, poor man deathwards go together.

That is the truth that the true poet, like the mariner who knows tomorrow's wind, must bear in mind. The second example evolves from the statement that poetry seduces our minds. A shift is made from poet to his public, and Ajax is cited as an example of the public's blinded understanding.

We might pause for a moment to notice how bizarrely Pindar argues. "Odysseus," he says, "wasn't as good as Homer said. That was Homer's fault because poetry misleads. We don't understand it; that's our fault. For example, we misunderstood Ajax." The argument is an example of pre-rational logic; we anticipate an order that is never realized. Indeed, the mention of Ajax plays back with special resonance on the criticism of Homer, for it is the overesteem paid to Odysseus that gave him the weapons of Achilles and led to Ajax' dishonored death. Logically, however, Ajax is not an example of the poet's fault; he is the illustration of the public's incomprehension. That is to say, the two steps of the argument coalesce in the poet's dissatisfaction with his predecessor. The dissatisfaction, however, yields to still darker considerations. The earlier statement of the death that awaits both rich and poor is reechoed; not even poetry can save us from annihilation:

> Hades' universal
> Wave comes on, falls on unfamed
> And on famed.

Not only, then, is poetry hazardous in that both the communicator and receptor are flawed, but the vanity of human existence makes the effort to write true poetry for the ideal audience idle. This is the truth that the wise man poet, the mariner, knows.

On recule pour mieux sauter. The girandole shines best from darkness. For the paradigms of Odysseus and Ajax is substituted Neoptolemos, whose death is sanctified:

> But worshiped are they whose history
> Tenderly god will magnify, delivering
> From death.

In place of the logos about Odysseus, the history that was in the poet's trust, we have now the intimation of some higher keeping, the logos that god protects. The events leading to Neoptolemos' mysterious death at Delphi are quickly treated. The narrative ends with the institution of his hero-cult. Neoptolemos, however, is not the subject of this eulogy. He but plays a part in the argument that will lead to the praise of Sogenes, Pindar's patron. The mention, then, of the hero-cult at Delphi recalls the statement in the ode's beginning section that the Aeacids watch over, as beneficent influences, the actions of their relative, the present athlete. And the present athlete's victory entails the poet's debt to sing his excellence:

> Let one compete and win: he casts
> In Music's current a theme, a honey to my mind;
> For exploits lacking hymns go darkly;

> One way alone we know to mirror actions' beauty:
> By diamond diademed Memory's grace if labor's
> Recompense be found, the singer's eulogy.

So much had been cliché, brilliantly ornamented, but still the commonplace. It had been Pindar's meditation on the dangers inherent in his attempt to satisfy this debt that induced his reflection on the three paradigms —Odysseus, Ajax, and Neoptolemos. In Neoptolemos, as we have said, he found the possible indication of a way out of the ephemeral. Pindar is now ready to begin the subject of Sogenes, but he must first turn away from Neoptolemos and place him, too, in the background. He does this by a variation of the break-off formula. He will not tell the story of Neoptolemos from its beginning:

> Few words —no more—
> Suffice to do his good name justice: I stand no liar
> To testify, Aegina, to the acts that your and Zeus's
> Breed have done. Dare I narrate
> The shining excellence, the lordly road
> Of words from first to last? —but no!
> Surcease . . . ! how pleasant in any occupation!
> Honey and the joy flowers of love, these even
> Cloy.

His statement that he is no liar is, of course, his challenge to Homer and to poetry in general, whose tinkling lies mislead. He cannot, then, blithely praise his patron. He returns to the subject of the opening invocation. Life, like his poem, is beset with dangers. To survive childhood and arrive at adolescence, we need the aid of Eleithyia, who acts with the Destinies or Fates to make us what we are:

> for want of you
> Not light, not black night is seen,
> Nor is she ours, your sister, Youth and lustrous limbs.

Her dispensations, however, are not equal. Greatness is a coordinate of the inequality of our birth:

> Diversities of fate enjoin our own diversity.

Sogenes, then, had emerged in this first crescendo of the ode as divinely blessed. He had, through the beneficence of Eleithyia, the Destinies, and the Aeacids, achieved a pinnacle of brilliance; and this moment of excellence demanded, as we have said, poetry to give it permanence. Now, after the aria-like meditation on poetry, Pindar resumes the opening themes, colored, however, by the burden of the dangers that beset his task. This second crescendo will occupy the remainder of the ode and will present his patron's possible escape from vicissitude and meaningless death. And it will do this, as we shall see, by a certain vibrancy, established in the already stated themes, which invites our minds to hazard that intuitive flight beyond the power of words to grasp what has not been said.

Each item of the eulogy must be kept in perfect balance. Sogenes' family is fortunate but fortune can change. Too much happiness almost invites disaster; too little is not happiness. Thearion, the father of Sogenes, is at the very dividing-point, the "crisis of stability." Nor is he by ambition apt to off-set the delicate balance. We should not be surprised that this enduring moment of felicity is both outside the individual's control and yet something for which he is personally responsible; it belongs to the multiple vision of mythopoeic thought to accept simultaneously logically contradictory postulates. Pindar must in his poetry achieve this same stable crisis. Exorbitant praise invites criticism:

> Look! I am your friend. I hold at bay
> The shadows of reproach, like streams
> Of water bring you very praise.

It is thus that he resumes the theme cast in music's current, and his own high obligation. But he has turned from Neoptolemos, and now, in an elaborate conceit, he again sees that

hero placed in the background; even a kinsman of Neoptolemos, however, would not reproach the poet for his new
theme:

> What man from overseas, what Achaean from Ionia —
> Let him come!— would blame me?

For Pindar has a special impulsion to sing of Sogenes; he is
an honorary citizen of Aegina and he is known amongst the
people for his balanced conduct:

> Who knows will say
> If beyond my range I go in converse out of tune.

By another brilliant conceit he recalls the break-off formula
itself. He did not —indeed, will not— compose an epic tale,
the lordly road from first to last, for such would be out of his
sphere as lyric poet. And yet the action of Sogenes was in its
way out of its sphere, for he won the pentathlon by competing
victoriously in but the first three —or four— of the five
events:

> I swear I did not overstep
> My sphere, nor hurl my song like bronze,
> The barbèd javelin that freed your brawn
> Of neck from wrestling's sweat before
> Your body felt the burning sun.

If Pindar had really "mirrored actions' beauty," he would
have gone beyond his sphere. Sogenes, therefore, no less than
Neoptolemos, is given the high accolade of an epic *recusatio*.
Notwithstanding, a debt exists. The poet must hazard poetry:

> Let me rejoice the victor, even were I
> To shout in exaltation: I pay my debts!

The task suddenly seems easy, and he, now near the end
of the ode, begins his song:

> Rhythm! Music!
> My Muse infixes gold on elephantine white
> With lily gathered from the sea's foam-flower.

The object described is the lyric crown, the object found through diamond-diademed Memory's grace. By memory one remembers what has happened and records it in a form that is memorable. That is poetry. But this is less and more: less in that the action of Sogenes is now not recorded, more in that the poet sees or foresees his poem's performance and the presentation of a crown. He shifts persona and speaks as, or with, the chorus of Aeginetan singers. He takes his place in their citizenry. The burden of the ode now is to place his patron's logos in the keeping of beneficent deities, Zeus and Athena, and, more particularly, in the keeping of heroes or saints, those who have made the transformation from mortal to immortal: Aeacos and Heracles. A mention of the latter suggests a new conceit. Just as the tomb of Neoptolemos neighbors the contests fought at Delphi —and therefore that hero's influence is felt by an Aeginetan competitor there, —so Sogenes, on Aegina, lives in a house neighbored by the sanctuary of Heracles:

> Look! the thill parts the harnessed
> Four-in-hand: just so to right and left
> Their house is bounded by your sanctuary.

Heracles as neighbor will intercede with deity. Pindar has placed Sogenes in the convergence of forces that will lead him to salvation out of the impasse of human frailty. The poem had begun with the powers that brought Sogenes to the moment of his greatness at Nemea. It ends with the powers that will bring him and his line beyond death. But what has not been cannot be spoken. This true poetry goes beyond the syntax of language; it bypasses the vagaries of an audience and propitiates the cosmic forces that will receive the poet's trust.

In the background stand the dangers passed, not only the vicissitudes of existence but the various false enticements of poetry. The poet has not written epic. Neoptolemos will not blame him. Nor will Sogenes, who in this crescendo appears against the paradigm of Neoptolemos. Pindar's poetry itself achieves transcendent place at the end of the ode, for what had been the object of his dissent now reappears unveiled, the pure mnemonic phrase, the piece of propaganda, the sentence from a catechism:

> Nonsense
> To recommence, to rattle on and on the text:
> "Who made you?" "God."

NEMEA VII: For Sogenes of Aegina, Boy Pentathlete

ΕΛΕΙΘΤΙΑ ΠΑΡΕΔΡΕ ΜΟΙΡΑΝ ΒΑΘΥΦΡΟΝΩΝ

Recitative

STROPHE

Eleithyia, coadjutrix of Destinies *en séance,*
And child of Majesty, of Hera —oyez!—
O Genetrix of birth: for want of you
Not light, not black night is seen,
Nor is she ours, your sister, Youth and lustrous limbs.
Yet inbreathe do we life not all the same:
Diversities of fate enjoin our own diversity. So yours
Especial is Thearion's son judged for merit,
Sung illustrious Sogenes, pentathlete.

ANTISTROPHE

For he dwells where dance is loved, in the city
Of lancer Aeacids, zealots to promote
Enthusiasts, their peers experient in Contest.
Let one compete and win: he casts
In Music's current a theme, a honey to my mind;

For exploits lacking hymns go darkly;
One way alone we know to mirror actions' beauty:
By diamond diademed Memory's grace if labor's
Recompense be found, the singer's eulogy.

Aria

EPODE

The poets know what wind is three days
Off and unmarred are by avarice:
Rich man, poor man deathwards go
Together. Yet I expect
Odysseus' history greater than the fact
Through Homer's verbal charm,

STROPHE

For in his fictions and contrivèd soar there is
An awesome something: Poetry is thief,
Through myth seductress of our minds; the public,
In the large, has a blinded sensitivity. Were it
To know the truth . . . then wroth for the arms had Ajax
Strong not fixed his entrails on the polished
Sword (whom, the strongest save Achilles, the breath of
    Zephyr's
Convoy brought in swiftest ships to Ilium
To get the wife of blond-red Menelaus

ANTISTROPHE

Back). What of it? Hades' universal
Wave comes on, falls on unfamed
And on famed. But worshiped are they whose history
Tenderly god will magnify, delivering
From death. To wit: He lies ensepulchred in Pythia's
Plain by the Great Navel of Earth,
Our Foison, where he had come, Neoptolemos. With Priam's
    city sacked

(O Danaid ordeal!), off he sailed for Scyros,
Missed it; they wandered finally to Ephyra.

EPODE

In Molossia he ruled as king a little
While —which dignity in perpetuity
His line bears— went thence to his god,
Bringing from Troy her choicest
Treasures. And there the man knifed him
As they quarreled for the meats of sacrifice.

STROPHE

Great the chagrin of his Delphic hosts,
Though he but fulfilled what had to be:
"An Aeacid prince henceforth in the ancient
Grove by god's stone-solid mansion
Must abide in residence, the President of Sacrifice and
    Protocol
For the Pomp of Heroes."

                         Few words —no more—
Suffice to do his good name justice: I stand no liar
To testify, Aegina, to the acts that your and Zeus's
Breed have done. Dare I narrate

ANTISTROPHE

The shining excellence, the lordly road
Of words from first to last? —but no!
Surcease . . . ! how pleasant in any occupation!
Honey and the joy flowers of love, these even
Cloy.

Recitative (Reprise)

             Intrinsically each we differ: this lot
In life is yours, this yours. But who
For his own can seize the all of happiness? I cannot say
For whom Destiny has made that dispensation firm.
Yet your prosperity, Thearion, she poises

204

Nemea VII

At the crisis of stability: nor shall ambition
Distort your mind's lucidity.
Look! I am your friend. I hold at bay
The shadows of reproach, like streams
Of water bring you very praise:
This wage accords with excellence.

STROPHE

What man from overseas, what Achaean from Ionia —
Let him come!— would blame me? Am I not a citizen
Here *honoris causa*? I walk
Amongst your people with a level gaze,
Unpretentiously, spurning excess: may future time
Continue in benevolence! Who knows will say
If beyond my range I go in converse out of tune.
Euxenid-sired, O Sogenes, I swear I did not overstep
My sphere, not hurl my song like bronze,

ANTISTROPHE

The barbèd javelin that freed your brawn
Of neck from wrestling's sweat before
Your body felt the burning sun.
A struggle, yes, but pleasure more
Than compensates. Let me rejoice the victor, even were I
To shout in exaltation: I pay my debts.
To intertwine a verbal crown —how easy! Rhythm! Music!

Chorale

MY MUSE INFIXES GOLD ON ELEPHANTINE WHITE
WITH LILY GATHERED FROM THE SEA'S FOAM-FLOWER.

EPODE

For Nemea, mention Zeus. (Soft
Strike our chorused voices'
Psalmody; this ground resound —as fits

The King of gods— *ma dolce*
E piano.) He planted in the womb, our history
Says, the seed of Aeacos,

STROPHE

Our noble country's founding prince
And, O Heracles, your toward friend
And brother. A friend in deed . . . a neighbor,
So might we say, whose mind intends
His neighbor's love, is a delightful joy, a nonpareil.
But if a god should play that role . . . ? Why
Then Sogenes, a son in his father's house, would live —how
     good
His luck!— near you (who over Giants triumphed)
In his family's sacred avenues of opulence:

ANTISTROPHE

Look! the thill parts the harnessed
Four-in-hand: just so to right and left
Their house is bounded by your sanctuary. O
Most Holy, intercede with Hera's lord
And the daughter whose eyes are agate. For yours is the gift
Of our salvation out of the impasse of our frailty.
We pray: weave in consonance his life firm founded
Fortunate in youth and in the splendency of age. And may
His childrens' children have forever

EPODE

This present prize or greater still.
My heart will never say
I wounded Neoptolemos with thoughtless words.
That field is plowed! Nonsense
To recommence, to rattle on and on the text:
"Who made you?" "God."

PYTHIA IX: "Come Then, My Pomp and Splendor of the Shade"

The god Apollo ravished to the open sunlight of Africa his
bride, Cyrene, the nymph he found lurking in the shadows of
the Thessalian north. At basis, the myth recalls, no doubt,
some historical migration of Greeks south to a colony across
the Mediterranean; and its expression as another instance of
the "stolen bride" theme shows the typical deflection of real
event toward the folklore patterns, existent in the earliest
literature, or rather, pre-literature, that recall the time when
men thought in a language close to dreams. Thus, unconsciously, reality, as it was recorded and remembered through
successive generations, was transmuted into its generic types.
So also, for example, was Helen to mask with her feminine
beauty the hard fact that the Greeks went to Troy perhaps to
steal the treasure guarded in the royal palace. Through the
normal processes, therefore, by which language and thought
develop, history was falsified and the higher truth of poetry
evolved. The generic type, it must be admitted, obscures
particular diversity; and the classicism of fifth-century
Greece, as it attempts to define the individual and his ulti-

mate truth, will be magnificently hampered by the archetypal language of the tradition.

But Pindar does not anticipate his century's interest in the individual. He, like his contemporary, Aeschylus, still hears, although with climactic complexity, the reverberations the old themes strike in his mind. His vision is double and triple, like the phenomenon obtained when several similar but different transparencies are superimposed and projected on the same screen. The outline is blurred, and from the confusion emerges a transcendent Gestalt. Rather than focus on the individual, on just one of the slides, he subjects that image to the total truth, burying it beneath some emerging hieratic pose common to them all, one that will have for him the greater metaphysical significance. The technique or process of thought had already occurred in Homer. When Achilles, for example, fights the river Xanthus, he is Achilles the hero superimposed upon the heavenly fire of lightning, the iconographical attribute of Zeus, his patron. The river, too, is water first, then man or god. The combat at times is but the ultimate example of other battles in the *Iliad*; at times, however, the elemental transformations dominate, and the river, a real river, dammed by the accumulation of dead bodies, overflows its banks and floods the plain. Now, if Achilles is to die, he will not die slain by the sword, but faces the danger of simply drowning. And, as the lens again refocuses, he is seen as Hephaestos and as that god's fire. Elemental fire fights with water, and it all becomes simplified in the simile comparing the battle to the homely cauldron overflowing onto the fire beneath it.

Cyrene, Apollo's bride, is of course a city in Africa, a colony of Greek civilization planted there in that "Third Continent." She thus has three very easy imagistic transformations: the woman, the plant, and the city. None of these is in itself exceptionally original, for the woman is not uncommonly thought of as the receptacle of the male seed, and the eponymous deity often reemerges from the topography to assume an independent existence. Thus, for example, Athens is Athens and also Athena. It is the extreme delicacy with which Pindar manipulates this confusion in the poem he wrote for Telesicrates that produces that poem's tender beauty. The Pythian victory is a crown that will be dedicated to the city of Cyrene. But if the city can wear a crown and if, moreover, she is given the epithet "equestrienne," she is on the verge of the transformation which, by the simple addition of a relative pronoun, will be precipitated as she appears in her role as Apollo's bride. But even as woman, she maintains the ambience of her other natures which suffuse her feminine persona. The short statement of the myth —for the second treatment will be much more extensive— ends in a haze of multiple perceptions; Apollo's queen is the choice plant brought to a new fertile land, one that will grow into a city, a continent:

> . . . . and where the plains
> Are fertile and fertile pastures, her, queen, implanted,
> Root of the Third Continent, to dwell, beloved, to
>   flourish.

But the act of implanting is a doublet for the sexual act, for Aphrodite is at hand to welcome the chariot from Delos and to change the ravished into the consenting bride.

Before repeating the myth with fuller coloration, the ode plunges backward in time, first to Cyrene's father, Hypseus, then to his birth by the naiad Creousa, who, in this most ancient temporal nucleus, is revealed as the daughter of Earth. Cyrene therefore has genealogical right to her chthonian attributes.

Time is retraced and Cyrene is born to begin the more luxuriant *più adagio* narrative of her life in the poem. She is a mixture of pastoral guardian and Amazon; and as she wanders through the wind valleys of Mount Pelion, she is seen by Apollo, who calls to the beast-man, Chiron, the Centaur, to gain his approval of the love which the sight of

Cyrene has inspired. The language again —and this time it
is Apollo's; he, as the Centaur will most eloquently point out,
is prophetic— endows Cyrene with her plant-like attributes:

> Who is she? Whose daughter? A cutting from what plant
> That here she lurks in shade of mountains
> For bravura trial of strength?
> Would Nature scruple? . . . Might I put
> This sacred hand on her? Bed her? Mow the sweetness
> Of her grass?

The questions are superfluous, for Apollo, who knows all,
knows, in this poem particularly, the elements of the land-
scape; he knows:

> . . . . the be-all
> And the end-all and all the ways,
> Every leaf the vernal earth puts forth,
> How many sands in the seas and rivers
> The waves and beats of the winds
> Churn, what
> Will be and whence.

But Chiron, to indulge the god's amorous fancy, does indeed
contend with him in revelation. His prophecy elaborates the
earlier-mentioned planting of the root of the third continent,
for it is now said that this act will take place in the "especial
garden of Zeus." And Africa herself appears as woman, mar-
velously endowed with "breadth of prairies" and "gold
demesnes" to welcome Apollo and his bride:

> . . . . she grants in perpetuity a tract of land where
> tillage
> Fails not the varied harvest nor the hunt abundant
> game.

Cyrene, who delighted in the hunt, has now become, with her
land-grant, the land itself, and the game-preserve. Fertile
Cyrene will there conceive and bequeath to a child the full

treasure of her pastoral attributes; for her child, the agrarian deity Aristaeos, will return to his great-great-grandmother, Earth, and taste the food of immortality:

Hermes, to the Hours' high throne
And Earth, shall take the mother's child
To dandle on their knees and be the idol of their eyes.
With nectar on his lips and droplets of ambrosia, immortal,

A Zeus, will they make him,
Or Apollo, the holy: humanity's delight, a close,
Most constant shepherd of flocks;
His name shall be 'Huntsman' and 'Pastor'; still others shall
    say him 'Aristaeos.'

As phophecy quickly passes into reality, the Cyrene-narrative is abridged; and the lovely woman is refocused and reappears as the city, glorified by Telesicrates' success. She has been enriched by the burden of the narrative, however, and she too, like the Lady Libya, stands in welcome, not of Apollo, but of another cortège from Delos, that of Telesicrates and the glory he brings "to his land where women flower."

The narrative has an iridescent life of its own as Cyrene in her multiple forms convinces us of her beauty, not because of particular physical qualities, but because of the pomp and splendor, the vegetative luxuriance of her metamorphoses. It would be idle to inquire, as we do perhaps in novels, about the psychological veracity of Pindar's portrait. We cannot deny that Apollo and Chiron's bantering about the relative virtues of rape and seduction provides a light tone, but it is all in the service of the narrative's total lyricism and does not ask us to pause for the individual personality. In the same way, a play of Aeschylus is weakened if the critic sees the stage-figure as a living psychological entity, rather than as a larger metaphorical coalescence in the service of the tragedy's poetic communication.

The leisurely narrative of Cyrene was, as we have seen, abridged, and the return to Telesicrates marked the completion of the ode's first movement. The second movement begins with a comment which is at once both an explanation of the previous break-off technique and a manifesto of the poet's manner:

> Excellence extraordinary is a fertile theme:
> But a detail is selected to ornament
> For an audience of cognoscenti: just so, proportion
> Is ever primest precept.

This statement must be understood in relation to the entire ode's structure. The armature that Pindar here uses is that of the simple victory catalog; he expands the form by ornamenting, always in a different style, although perhaps in a common tonality, the simple recording of items in a list. The Pythian victory, the most recent and the one which supplies the occasion for the poem, is mentioned first. "The Pythic shield bronze victory," or the race run in armor at Delphi, receives a fairly traditional development, ending with the mention of the victor's city. This detail, then, Cyrene, is selected for the narrative expansion that we have just discussed. That the narrative had been lengthy justified the poet's use of the break-off formula to complete that section of the poem.

To mark the transition to the second item in the catalog, Pindar therefore states first that for each triumph there is much that he could write; and yet, since his audience is well versed in the techniques of lyrical panegyric, he will present to them not the full account but the brilliant expansion of a single detail. This was, as they will no doubt note, what the myth of Cyrene had performed. He could, if he so wished, as fully ornament the second item in the catalog; however,—and this is his second point,—proportion is of the utmost importance. The victory at Delphi was more recent and therefore paramount. The other items must recede so as not to detract from the primacy of Delphi. Not only is this matter of the relative importance of the victories true, however, but Pindar is doubtless saying that in order for his poem to produce total aesthetic satisfaction, it must vary its manner, and slow narrative must yield to scherzo.

The games of Iolaos at Thebes form the second item in the catalog, but the matter is so tangentially broached that we must indeed be among the cognoscenti —as in fact the ancient scholars who attempted to explain the passage were not— to recognize the melody beneath the agréments. In illustration of Pindar's manifesto and incidentally in parody of the Cyrene myth, Iolaos, again by the addition of a relative pronoun, is selected as the theme for the this-time whirlwind narrative. The elements in the story are so quickly touched upon that comprehension is almost lost. The events remain obscure, but apparently Iolaos, who was the son of Iphicles, Heracles' twin brother, killed Eurystheus —who had been persecuting Heracles' children— and then was buried (either because he was dead or because in this manner he would be rejuvenated) in the tomb of his grandfather Amphitryon, who had come to Thebes and died. Amphitryon, in turn, is now selected as the detail; and the narrative begins again with the adultery of Zeus with Amphitryon's wife Alcmene, and the subsequent birth of twins: Heracles, the son of Zeus; and Iphicles, the son of Amphitryon.

The Iolaos myth is Theban material and, as such, has special relevance for the Theban poet, Pindar. The whole ornamentation of the second item of the victory catalog comes to a climax in the mention of Heracles and the Theban spring, Dirce, whose waters Pindar habitually uses as a metaphor for his poetry. The climax, in fact, turns out to be a most subtle transition to the remaining items in the catalog, for the poet has just displayed two virtuoso pieces, a long and a short narrative, and he now feigns that he faces the danger of hav-

ing no more to give, no new manner of approach. Heracles
and Dirce, then, stand as a native source of inspiration; to
them he prays to find more words:

> This prayer to them be answered;
> Sing: leave me never,
> Purity of light, cadenza of you Elegancies!

The prayer is answered and more items are added to the list:
three victories at Aegina and a victory at the Ridge of Nisos
or Megara. The coloration this time is that the successes are
the "victorious flight from silence attendant/ On defeat." The
victor has a right to boast; the poet has a right to praise him.
Even an enemy —real, perhaps, but more probably the straw-
man enemy of the cliché— will have to render him justice.

The erotic element, so evident in the first movement, is
latent in the famous adultery of Zeus and Alcmene, and begins to emerge as the second movement draws to its close; for
the group of enemies and friends who must render the victor
justice almost imperceptibly recalls the welcoming scenes of
the first movement. The next item in the catalog brings the
erotic clearly to the forefront; at the games in Athens, the
victor's beauty inspires in the spectators thoughts of love:

> I saw you often victor
> In the yearly rites of Pallas —
> And speechless every
> Woman prayed,
> O Telesicrates, you be her husband or her son.

The final items, the games of Earth and those at Cyrene,
bring us back to the ambiguous haze in which a woman is
also land:

> .... the Games of Earth —whose drapery
> Is her valleys— and all your country's
> Contests.

There is, however —for so the third movement begins—
another element proper to the victory catalog, and that is

some mention of other victors in the patron's family. The movement boldly announces the subject as simply a subject, but its wording also recalls the cliché of Dirce's waters, and we are asked to expect perhaps still another varied treatment:

> And while I quench our thirst
> For song, there comes someone to make me wake
> Another debt, your forebears' ancient glory.

We have seen that the second movement had modulated back to the tonality of the first movement and Cyrene; we are now presented with a companion-piece to that narrative. Again a courtship is the theme and again the language confuses woman and vegetative luxuriance:

> O golden crown of Youth,
> O ripening grain! You
> Would they harvest. To cultivate his daughter a brilliant
> Marriage, her father recalled . . . .

The story recalled is that of Danaos and his troupe of daughters, whom he paired off with the sons of Aegyptos by means of a race. Antaeos uses the same method to choose his daughter's husband. It is Alexidamos, an ancestor of Telesicrates, and apparently a victor in the games, who gets the bride and is saluted for his triumph:

> Leaves and wreaths
> They cast —like his former victories' plumes.

Thus the poem ends, but the finale rouses new images that play upon the earlier material in our minds.

———————

Alexidamos, who had before raced for victory, races in Libya for his bride. His essence as racer invites us to place his image upon the victor, Telesicrates, and he is perhaps even awarded, at the end of the poem, the elements of the crown which Telesicrates at the beginning will present to Cyrene.

It has been suggested that Telesicrates, like Alexidamos and Apollo, is bringing home a real bride. The interpretation is an error of the biographical approach to poetry, but it testifies to a subtle perception that would be true were it not false. It is false, of course, because a metaphor does not prove a real event, but it is true because the multiple vision does refocus on Telesicrates. He is given the hieratic pose of his other personae, and as he arrives in Africa to be greeted by the assembled people, he is indeed like Apollo greeted first by Aphrodite and then by that goddess's transformation, as it were, into the Lady Libya. The bride that Telesicrates brings home is victory, and the erotic metaphor radiates from the eyewitness account Pindar gives us of the effect Telesicrates had upon those who saw him perform.

Pythia IX: For Telesicrates of Cyrene: Victory in the Race Run in Armor

---

ΕΘΕΛΩ ΧΑΛΚΑΣΠΙΔΑ ΠΤΘΙΟΝΙΚΑΝ

FIRST MOVEMENT

ouverture

(strophe)

My will the Pythic shield bronze
Victory —O second it, your Elegancies
In Empire gowns— proclaims, the man
Of fortune, Telesicrates, the coronal of equestrienne
    Cyrene:

moderato

Whom Leto's crinèd son once ravished from the
    shrieking
Wind valleys
Of Mount Pelion and brought on gold the rustic
    huntress —
On chariot; and where the plains
Are fertile and fertile pastures, her, queen, implanted,

Root of the Third Continent, to dwell, beloved, to
flourish.

(antistrophe)
In welcome argent-sandaled Aphrodite touched
Her guest from Delos' chariot,
Which god had made: her hand was light,
The spell of tenderness upon their bed of love
She cast, inducing to consent to god the daughter
Of sovereign Hypseus,

vivace

Then King of the militant Lapiths, second
In the generations of Heroes from Ocean:
Born in one of Pindos' legendary valleys where
The Naiad Creousa, Earth's daughter, indulged her
pleasure

(epode)
In Peneios' bed.
And their son raised
A child of his own,

moderato ma più adagio (reprise)

Cyrene, so lovely of limb, who scorned
The tedious pacing
At her loom or meals with housewife stay-at-homes;
But javelins of bronze or sword —
These were her tools: she fought and slew
Wild beasts, brought peace
And quiet to her father's herds;
She'd rise at dawn-break,
Sated with the pleasures
Of her bedmate, Sleep —or rather, Nap.

(strophe)
Look! She was wrestling bare-handed and alone
A marauding lion when he saw her —
His arrows ensheathed which cosmic rain,

Pythia IX

Apollo, I mean. "Chiron!" he called. "Philyra's
Son, come out! Leave your holy cave;
Come see this wonder,
A woman who fights and wins —and such quarrel
She's picked! What stamina the lady
Has! Her mind to calm turns winter fears.
Who is she? Whose daughter? A cutting from what plant

(antistrophe)

That here she lurks in shade of mountains
For bravura trial of strength?
Would Nature scruple? . . . Might I put
This sacred hand on her? Bed her? Mow the sweetness
Of her grass?" Not frown, but genial burst of laughter
As the Centaur disabused him:
"Hidden in sophistics of Seduction are the keys to
    sacraments
Of love, O Phoebos. Both
Gods and men are shamed and blush at this: without
Preamble, rushing in to take the pleasures of a virgin's
    bed.

(epode)

The blandishments of lust induced that nonsense
You just spoke —lies from you are out of character. You
    ask
Her parentage, her background,
King? You? . . . who know the be-all
And the end-all and all the ways,
Every leaf the vernal earth puts forth,
How many sands in the seas and rivers
The waves and beats of the winds
Churn, what
Will be and whence.
Must I contend with you in revelation?

(strophe)

So be it. Her husband-to-be you enter this clearing,

And across the sea to the especial
Garden of Zeus shall you bear her away;
There will you crown her: Metropolis of an island people
Assembled on a rising of plain-girt land. Look!
The Lady Libya
In her breadth of prairies joyously welcomes your
    eminent
Bride to her gold demesnes;
Now she grants in perpetuity a tract of land where tillage
Fails not the varied harvest nor the hunt abundant game.

(antistrophe)

There your son will be born: Saint
Hermes, to the Hours' high throne
And Earth, shall take the mother's child
To dandle on their knees and be the idol of their eyes.
With nectar on his lips and droplets of ambrosia,
    immortal,
A Zeus, will they make him,
Or Apollo, the holy: humanity's delight, a close,
Most constant shepherd of flocks;
His name shall be 'Huntsman' and 'Pastor'; still others
    shall say him 'Aristaeos.' "
Such words urged on the consummation of the joyous
    rites of marriage.

(epode)

Swift what gods have will to do
Is done: their ways are short. That that day brought
To pass: he slept
In Libya's gold-rich chamber —loveliest

ouverture (reprise)

Of cities in the Games his protégée,
Which now at Pytho the Sacrosanct is celebrate
In Carneiades' son's success,
His victory, the apotheosis of Cyrene.
With *allegresse* she welcomes him

220

And the glory he brings
From Delphi to his land where women flower.

SECOND MOVEMENT: *scherzo*

(strophe)

(Excellence extraordinary is a fertile theme;
But a detail is selected to ornament
For an audience of cognoscenti: just so, proportion
Is ever primest precept.)

Iolaos, too,
Whom Thebes of Seven Gates had known, found
He was his peer. (Ah, Iolaos:
Who was hidden —Eurysthenes decapitated— beneath
   the earth
In the tomb where his grandfather Amphitryon,
Charioteer and envoy of the Spartans, buried lay —
   burial
In alien residence, the avenues of Cadmos where the
   white horses trod.

(antistrophe)

And Amphitryon: to him and Zeus Alcmene
Conceived —in innocence— and bore
To each his son, triumphant twins.
A man were dumb who not embrace this chance
To talk of Heracles nor mention always Dirce's
Waters, which nourished
Him and Iphicles.)

This prayer to them be answered;
Sing: leave me never,
Purity of light, cadenza of you Elegancies! Yes, I say,
Thrice he glorified his city at Aegina and the Ridge of
   Nisos,

(epode)

Victorious flight from silence attendant
On defeat. Therefore, if friend or civic enemy, what was
   done

For the commonweal refuse
To denigrate, as said the Old Man of the Sea:
"With all your heart and justice
Him praise, though enemy, who acted well."

I saw you often victor
In the yearly rites of Pallas —
And speechless every
Woman prayed,
O Telesicrates, you be her husband or her son—

(strophe)

And in the Olympics and the Games of Earth —whose
    drapery
Is her valleys— and all your country's
Contests.

THIRD MOVEMENT: *moderato cantabile*

    And while I quench our thirst
For song, there comes someone to make me wake
Another debt, your forebears' ancient glory:
To Irasa they came
For a Libyan bride, suitors for Antaeos' daughter's
Ravishing éclat and splendid
Chevelure. So many princes of her blood asked for her
    hand;
And foreigners also many. Such a vision she was, a
    marvel

(antistrophe)

To see. O golden crown of Youth,
O ripening grain! You
Would they harvest. To cultivate his daughter a brilliant
Marriage, her father recalled how Danaos in Argos
Had found a way most swift, before high noon,
To marry off his forty-
Eight daughters: he placed his chorus of girls
At the finish line of a race.

"Run!" he said. "The contest will decide. Each of you
    men
Who came to seek a bride shall have whichever one you
    take."

(epode)

The Libyan thus to a husband matched
The daughter he gave away. At a mark he placed the
    girl,
Making her the goal;
Proclaimed in public, "Whoever rush there first
And touch her gown may take her."
Alexidamos then sprinted down the track,
Grasped with hand her cherished
Hand, and led her through the crowd
Of Nomad chevaliers.
Leaves and wreaths
They cast —like his former victories' plumes.

Olympia XI, Pythia XII, Olympia IV, Olympia XIV: Some Voluntaries and Panache

The shorter ode which, as Pindar himself would say, answered a particular occasion and its special need, could at times, despite the inescapable difficulties of its limited scope, achieve a unique tone—a brilliance like that of a trumpet voluntary, which, for all its éclat, strives for depth, too often in vain. The victor has won, and on the evening of his triumph, his entourage at the site of the games must celebrate him with carousal and extemporaneous panegyric. For the celebration, a poet, even on such short notice, might be asked to compose a formal salute. The commissioned work is obviously but a minor flourish when compared to the grand ovation at the formal banquet which will welcome the athlete home to his compatriots. The difficulty of the short ode was not merely the speed of its creation— the grandeur of Homer reminds us of what a poet can do in near-extemporaneous composition when he works with traditional material and language— but more the very shortness of the form. Pindar's poetry achieves its beauty, as we have seen, by a certain resonance that the thematic material assumes, as vision is imposed upon vision; the end of the poem invites us to reconsider in memory the beginning; and the totality rings on into more transcendent visions which surpass the simple statement. The linear time of the ode's performance plays against our mental impression of concentricity. If, as in the brief ode, time is too short, our impression is of isolated splendors that lack coherence. It is paradoxical that this same failing occurs also in the longer odes of Pindar that we have omitted to translate. In these odes, apparently, the theme was not of resonant metal and yet the poet was too much a professional to refuse to write, merely for lack of inspiration.

And yet the leap to the infinite is, as we have learned from the haiku, not impossible even from the most circumscribed ground. We are never quite sure, however, that the truncated statement really did invite us to soar. Or was it merely our imagination that saw too much where so little was meant? Our contemporary taste for this phenomenon was prepared for us by the imagists and finds satisfaction in the reading of fragments of the archaic and late archaic Greek poets. Appreciation and enjoyment are, of course, better than neglect; but no doubt the entire corpus, had it survived, would have pleased less, or in a different way. It would be easy, therefore, to convince one of Pindar's excellence, were we to make a selection from the fairly numerous fragments of his lost poems. Here it will be our task to see if Pindar, at times, wrote a short but full statement, a total ode, that yet produced an open-ended poem.

Despite the beauty of its opening section, the poem for Hagesidamos of Western Locris is the least successful of the four we have chosen to translate; and even the opening section is a not-too-eloquent elaboration of the cliché which claims that each thing has its due or need, or each person (as, for example, in the poem of Sappho) has his particular love. Three professions are selected: the navigator, the farmer, and the athlete; and each one needs something for him to prosper. The only magnificence is that implied by the parallelism which makes the athlete's panegyric comparable to the natural phenomena of wind and rain:

> Winds sometime are most
> Our need; or sometime heaven's waters,
> Showered daughters of the cloud.
> But here an athlete, trained, has won . . . him must hymns
> Of honey herald.

The conceit that at Olympia there is stored a grand treasure of glory that the poet will dip into for the victor is a fairly pleasant way of varying the envy-cliché: no one could begrudge the victor "Olympia's grand salute." Moreover, not only is the poet willing, but he feels within him the power of god. The accolade is therefore made and the poet lapses into a bald statement of another cliché, that which invites the Muses to visit the victor's country, where they will receive an appreciative welcome. How could the Western Locrians do otherwise? It is their nature:

> Inborn nature cannot change, not fiery
> Fox, not roaring lion.

The poem thus ends with a reminiscence of the beast-fable, which is, however, too easily applicable for the poem to terminate in anything less than a full stop. To apply the term cliché to the various elements in the poem does not condemn it to insignificance; we have seen, for example, the cliché of the Muses' journey magnificently elaborated into a full ode in "Nemea III." The total impression here, however, is of flatness, or perhaps of mere proficiency. It is slick, a poem without asperities. We would like to think that the victory itself did not interest the poet, but even this consolation for the critic is belied by the survival of the poem Pindar wrote for the later formal celebration of this very victory, "Olympia

X." There, of course, Pindar had discovered the happy possibility of reverberation in his central image, the art of memory.

———————

"Olympia XI," as we have seen, was but the simple string-
ing-together in linear fashion of eulogistic commonplaces;
"Pythia XII" contains a narrative in cyclic structure and
therefore seems a short version of a major epinician ode. The
victor, Midas of Agrigentum, has won the competition for
solo flute. (This is the only poem of Pindar's that has survived
for an occasion other than an athletic contest, and it serves
to remind us that music was originally the prime event at
Delphi and that even athletics were viewed as a form of
dance or art.) The central section narrates the mythological
origin of a particular musical form that Midas had performed
in the competition, a "chaconne on diverse heads." The Greek
flute, unlike the modern flute, was voiced by reeds and re-
sembled more the Renaissance krummhorn or shawm than
the modern oboe, in that the reed apparently was not con-
trolled directly by the lips but was encased in a mouthpiece.
The tone, as for all these reed-instruments, was nasal, and as
unlike the modern flute as the rasping quality of Chinese
opera is unlike the sonority of Italian opera. It is indeed this
nasal quality of the flute which serves as the basis for the in-
vention-myth. Perseus had decapitated one of the Gorgons,
those monstrous women with snakes for hair. The others'
weeping lamentation mingles with the sound of the serpents'
hissing, and Athena, who was present, imitates the sound with
instruments and produces the chaconne-composition. This is
the story that in two installments, at the beginning and end of
the central section, frames a mention of a later event in
Perseus' life—his arrival at Seriphos with the head of Medusa, which turned to stone the islanders, as well as Polydectes, who had courted Danaë by force.

The cyclic structure of the myth invites us to expect a
final return to Midas at the close of the ode, an expectation

that influenced the ancient critics to apply with particular
reference the closing gnomic expression of life's vicissitudes:

> Win, but strive, else no man
> Wins. Today —ah, god can end
> It all. Flee? From what
> Must be? Yet . . .
> A future time, though casting your despair,
> Unhoped will give you this and forestall that.

The reference, it is claimed, was to the fact that Midas had
broken his mouthpiece in the competition and continued to
play his instrument in the manner of an oboe rather than a
shawm. Unfortunately, these critics could have used nothing
but wild conjecture as a basis for their view, and we are
forced to see the gnomic section as a coda-like ending that
does not return to Midas with particular reference. And yet
the cyclicity does almost demand a final reechoing. We will
never know if the effect of this ode —the unanswered structural expectation— was volitional or merely inept, the result
perhaps of the poet's youth, for the poem is one of the earliest
datable works in Pindar's corpus. If the latter view is correct,
the poem shows us a poet who has made a brilliant beginning
into his art but who has not yet complete control over all of
its elements. The introduction of Midas maintains a certain
verbal radiance, and the relevance of the myth is inescapable.
There is, moreover, a mastery in the references to the tangential aspects of the myth. The critic would like, in good
Aristotelian mode, to conclude that such beginnings must in-
evitably lead to greater complexities. Again, we are embarrassed; later poems, such as "Olympia XI," often show less
control or originality than this earliest of the odes.

"Olympia IV," for the victory that Psaumios of Camarina won
with his mule team, is a late poem and shows the same disputed relevance of the final section. Here, however, the touch

is firm. The poem ends with a tangential element in the story
of the Argonauts. On the journey to Phasis, the Argonauts
had stopped at Lemnos and dallied there for love of that hus-
bandless tribe. The item that Pindar narrates concerns a race
in armor which won for Erginos the affection and admi-
ration of the queen, Hypsipyle, who had before disdained the
man because of his apparent age:

The Lemnian women
Scorned his love —at first.
But then he won the race, all brazen in his armor,
And spoke thus to Hypsipyle when he came to get his crown:
"Well, here I am: you've seen me run!
And heart can equal legs.
Often the hair grows grey —too soon,
Belying a young man's age. . . ."

Ancient critics again sought particular relevance in the episode, in claiming that Psaumios was prematurely grey when
he won at Olympia; and again the idea can be but a wild
conjecture read out of the supposed statement in the poem
itself. If, of course, the conjecture were true —and one is
reminded of the lady who said of Wallace Stevens, "If the
poem doesn't mean *that,* what *does* it mean?"— the application would have been immediately perceived by an audience well aware of Psaumios' grizzled appearance; the poem
would thus end with as full a stop as "Olympia XI." Unlike
"Pythia XII," however, this poem is not composed in cyclic
structure, and there is therefore no expectation aroused for a
return to the opening subject. The relevance of the myth to
the preceding statement is that the poet will not lie about his
patron's greatness, for the truth will out. And that cliché was
the concluding comment to the particular praise of Psaumios'
personal and political character. It is true that the celebration
for the victory is termed "Light most late, far-shining burst
of sun's/Strength, excellence," but it is not at all certain that
Psaumios himself looked old. It is quite probable that it

means merely that his city, Camarina, may, as the poet says, at last awake to glory; that is to say, Camarina has been too long without its share of splendor. The myth that forms the final section, therefore, is perhaps a most ornate flourish in illustration of the cliché. Or it is perhaps a comment on long-sleeping Camarina. In either case it arouses pleasing reminiscences of the magnificent beginning of the poem.

At the games, the poet hears the thundering hoofs of the team of mules and it calls to mind another thundering—that on high, the attribute of Zeus whose games these at Olympia are. The Seasons have again revolved; the Hours have passed, dancing to the lyrist's songs; they summon him again to come to Olympia, again to bear witness at the contests:

> Charioteer on high, your team has hoofs of thunder —
> O Zeus: for again these are your Hours,
> That to my lyre dance, my dappled song,
> Who circle, who summon me
> Bear witness here at this highest of Contests.

Nothing else in the poem equals the beauty of this invocation —and this lack is indeed a flaw. But the opening has established a tonality of time-consciousness, and the myth leaps over its context to rejoin in tone, though not in sense, the opening. The very extravagance of the myth with relation to its insignificant commonplace context indeed facilitates its disjoining. The poem achieves a certain expansion in our minds beyond the justifiable fanfare of the simple salute.

———————

The finest of the four short odes we have selected is also one of the earliest, written just two years later than the first datable poems of Pindar. There is a tension in "Olympia XIV" between the éclat of the voluntary and the somber tones the ode assumes in its last verses. No poem is so gentle; none more simple. (It is the poem generally chosen to introduce Pindar to a reader whose knowledge of Greek is somewhat limited.) The structure is a linear elaboration of the prayer-formula. The deity, in the general form of this genre, is addressed, is identified by several attributes (apparently originally for magical reasons, because language correctly phrased captured the will of deity), and finally, is asked to grant some particular favor. Sappho's invocation to Aphrodite, for example, is an instance of an especially successful treatment of this structure: in that poem, the poetess mocks herself; she has so often prayed to the goddess of love that the deity already knows what ails her—"Who is it this time," as she says, "wrongs you?" Pindar's poem, entirely different in its treatment, deserves to stand beside that other masterpiece.

The deities addressed are the group of Elegancies or Graces:

Partage of the Cephisos
Waters your site where colts so fine run,
O Queens, you singing Elegancies
Of shimmering Orchomenos, surveillants of the ancient
    Minyans.

They are addressed because they are present in all splendor, all beauty, human and divine. The heavenly festivities they superintend act as an image imposed upon the present festivity to honor Asopichos, and thus give it a heightened dimension. The reason for the celebration is stated most simply: the victor has added to the epithet of his nationality the word "Olympian." Although at first it had seemed that the Elegancies were asked merely to attend the revel, the particular request addressed to the deities evolves into a delicate conceit. The echo of the voices in the present ceremonies will travel, it is requested, to the underworld, where the victor's dead father will hear the news of his son's success:

. . . . Go, our Echo; reach
The black-walled mansion of Persephone; to his father
    there, Cleodamos,

Bring the news of victory; say:
"Your son has wreathed in the Pisan
Valley with wings of glory his youthful hair."

The echo, as heard in Hades, gives a second elaboration of
the earlier statement that Asopichos has gained the epithet
Olympian: that is to say, the echo sings with agréments; the
simple word "Olympian" stands out against the black-walled
mansion of Persephone and sets a fluttering radiance in
Hades.

Just as the image of heaven had exalted the present
regale, the plunging journey to Hades transforms the whole
to melancholy, immediately compensated for by joy. The
realms of Heaven, Earth, and Underworld, moreover, are
paralleled in the mention of Zeus on Olympus, the earthly
domains of the river Cephisos and the city Orchomenos, and
the somber palace of the dead. Resplendence, Merriment, and
Exuberance, who dance in heaven, dance in Orchomenos and
set up a dancing amongst the dead.

OLYMPIA XI: For Hagesidamos of Western Locris: Victory in Boxing, Boys' Division

ΕΣΤΙΝ ΑΝΘΡΩΠΟΙΣ ΑΝΕΜΩΝ ΟΤΕ ΠΛΕΙΣΤΑ

STROPHE

Winds sometime are most
Our need; or sometime heaven's waters,
Showered daughters of the cloud.
But here an athlete, trained, has won . . . him must hymns
Of honey herald. Preludes of his fame
To be, arise, and oath who swear his glory!

ANTISTROPHE

I broach —why not?— the treasure,
Olympia's grand salute. Tongue
Alone would shepherd words;
But more: for god inspires to flower my poet's talent.
Do hereby know, O Archestratos' son,
For boxing, Hagesidamos, panache, this music, on your crown

EPODE

Of olive gold
I sound;

And homage your tribe, the Western Locrians.
Join there their festival; I guarantee
You Muses find no lack of hospitality,
No boorish ignorance of beauty,
But warriors consummate and connoisseurs.
Inborn nature cannot change, not fiery
Fox, not roaring lion.

Pythia XII: For Midas of Agrigentum: Victory in the Solo Flute Competition

ΑΙΤΕΩ ΣΕ ΦΙΛΑΓΛΑΕ ΚΑΛΛΙΣΤΑ ΒΡΟΤΕΑΝ ΠΟΛΙΩΝ

STROPHE

Hear me, Desirant of Splendor, Metropolis Mortal of Beauty,
O Dais of Persephone! By the banks of Acragas, that pastures
Flocks, you dwell on citied hill, My Queen:
Be kind —immortals and men rejoice;
Take this Pythic crown, renownèd Midas';
Him take, champion of Greece
In Athena's art,
Pallas, who voices wove inventing
Brash Gorgons in funereal threnody,

STROPHE

Which to the drone of repellent snakes on their spinster heads
She heard, this libation of tears in an agony of sorrow:
One sister of the trio cut off and Perseus had taken
Her head as death to the islanders of Seriphos.
(Yes, he enshrouded the monstrous breed of Phorcys
And poisoned Polydectes' banquet

In vengeance for the slavery
His mother was enduring, her courtship by force.)
Medusa's "ravishing" head was the spoils

STROPHE

Danaë's son stripped (whom god unbidden rained
Begetting). Well, the virgin goddess saved
Her protégé from peril; devised the counterpoint of flutes
To imitate with instruments the cries of lamentation
Surfacing to lips from Euryale's rabid maw.
That was the deity's invention,
Given then
To men, named "Chaconne on Divers Heads,"
Which classic courts the nations to assemble

STROPHE

And streams through foil-beat bronze and voicing reeds
That, near the city where dance the Graces, grow
In the Cephisos marsh to modulate the dancers' steps.
Win, but strive, else no man
Wins. Today —ah, god can end
It all. Flee? From what
Must be? Yet . . .
A future time, though casting your despair,
Unhoped will give you this and forestall that.

OLYMPIA IV: Processional for Psaumios of Camarina: Victory With Chariot

ΕΛΑΤΗΡ ΥΠΕΡΤΑΤΕ ΒΡΟΝΤΑΣ ΑΚΑΜΑΝΤΟΠΟΔΟΣ

STROPHE

Charioteer on high, your team has hoofs of thunder —
O Zeus: for again these are your Hours,
That to my lyre dance, my dappled song,
Who circle, who summon me
Bear witness here at this highest of Contests.
A friend fares well; true friends rejoice,
And the news is sweet.
Ah yes, O Cronos' son, who lord Mount Aetna,
Windswept trap to clamp down storming hundred-headed
    Typho,
Consecrate your Olympic
Victor; grace these our revels —

ANTISTROPHE

Light most late, far-shining burst of sun's
Strength, excellence: Psaumios has come!
He is riding by; the olive of Pisa crowns him:

May Camarina awake
With him to glory; may god grant
Fulfillment to his prayers! Hear his eulogy: he has raised
A line of thoroughbreds;
Philanthropist, all strangers are his guests, his land asylum;
His motto: Peace, not Politics —Civic Concord, Patriotism!
No lie shall taint
My praise: No, for truth will out.

EPODE

It happened so with Clymenos' son.
The Lemnian women
Scorned his love —at first.
But then he won the race, all brazen in his armor,
And spoke thus to Hypsipyle, when he came to get his crown:
"Well, here I am: you've seen me run!
And heart can equal legs.
Often the hair grows grey —too soon,
Belying a young man's age. . . ."

OLYMPIA XIV: For Asopichos of Orchomenos: Victory in the Two-Hundred-Yard Dash

ΚΑΦΙΣΙΩΝ ΥΔΑΤΩΝ

STROPHE

Partage of the Cephisos
Waters your site where colts so fine run,
O Queens, you singing Elegancies
Of shimmering Orchomenos, surveillants of the ancient
   Minyans;
Hear: to you I pray whose presence is our joy;
And our delight your immanence in who is handsome,
Talented, let us say, or splendid man.
Nor even gods without you sacred Elegancies
Conduct their dances and regales. No: of all the heavenly
Festivities, intendants enthroned beside
Apollo Pythian Golden Bow,
You venerate our Olympian father's sempiternal majesty.

STROPHE

Lady, O Resplendence,
And Merriment, you lover of the dance, daughters to god

In the highest, attend me now,
And you, Exuberance, that yearn to dance: see
This cortège that for triumph nimbly steps,
Rehearsed in the Lydian mode I came
To sing Asopichos, who adds to Minyan
The epithet "Olympian." Go, our Echo; reach
The black-walled mansion of Persephone; to his father there,
     Cleodamos,
Bring the news of victory; say:
"Your son has wreathed in the Pisan
Valley with wings of glory his youthful hair."

Olympia X: The Interest Accrued

Upon the "places" in an imagined repository house of memory, the poet imprints iconographic transformations of the material to be remembered. Such is the "art of memory" which the Marmor Parium ascribes to Simonides. To remember, the poet walks through his house, reading off the pictures he had there written. Frances Yates (*The Art of Memory*, London, 1966) has shown us the long and involved life this technique has had in the Western tradition; but we are interested here in its original form as a simple rhetorical device. It provides the generative conceit for the ode Pindar composed for the Olympic victory of Hagesidamos of Western Locris. The poem had not, for whatever reason we do not know, been written immediately upon the victory; the poet pretends he had forgotten. But the very wording of the pretense belies his supposed critics' slanderous reproach, for the item of knowledge had already been codified and imprinted on the poet's mind; Pindar must now merely perform his corollary task, that of "deciphering" the impression.

But where in the house had Hagesidamos been placed? The answer to that question will indicate the high honor Pindar had granted his patron even before his ode had been composed; for Pindar, in a virtuoso display, is later in this poem to reproduce, with each hero's iconographic detail, the victory-catalog of the inaugural Games at Olympia. When at the beginning of his ode he reads the name of Archestratos' son, it is clear that this victor is but the latest entry in the full roster the preservation of which is the poet's sacred task. Hagesidamos had already been "placed," like the saints of a medieval cathedral, in his proper niche.

Indeed, the inaugural ceremonies are consciously confused with the present festivity. The first performance of the Games at Olympia culminated in an evening of revelry and the eulogistic celebration of the heroes:

> . . . . his comrades were fired
> To applaud. Evening, then.
> Ablaze. Moonlight.
> The beauty. And calm.
> Song all the sanctum filled in festivals
> Of revelry: the eulogy was born, ...

Had a poet not been present, the glory would have been transitory; the heroes would have "drawn breath only to strive / At emptiness for transitory joy." That Pindar has remembered them proves that theirs was no "sterile splendor" and therefore proves the worth of the praise the poet now offers to his patron. Since his name is inscribed on the victory-catalog, he presumably will form an item in some future poet's feat of memory.

The confusion of present and past paradigm is more extreme in the passage which introduces the central foundation-myth. Like the horn calls in the "Eroica," the new thematic subject is prematurely introduced, then startlingly curtailed: a mention of the battle of Heracles with Cycnos. In the first encounter, Heracles was defeated. The poet rapidly shifts to Hagesidamos' victory at Olympia, which is attributed to the excellence of his trainer, Ilas. By another rapid change,

Olympia X

Ilas and Hagesidamos are cast in the roles of Achilles and
Patroclos:

> To fight
> With Cycnos was too much
> For even Heracles: but then. . . A boxing victory
> At Olympia —thank Ilas,
> Hagesidamos; so Patroclos
> Did Achilles.

The meaning is conveyed entirely by implication. Heracles
won, of course, in the second encounter, but that is not stated;
instead, we have Hagesidamos' victory at Olympia. Perhaps
he too fought a return bout, but the startling juxtaposition
makes his victory seems Heracles'. Since the victor is young,
his success is at least partly a result of his training; again
Hagesidamos is cast in an ancient paradigm, for the trainer
and his protégé are like the classic lovers, Patroclos and Achilles. The homosexual nuance becomes clearer in the poem's
final transformation, when Pindar himself recalls the boy's
beauty and casts him as another Ganymede: Hagesidamos
has been saved from death by Pindar's poem, just as Zeus had
brought to heaven his favorite, Ganymede.

The anticipated theme of Heracles returns for fuller development in the mythic section. The theme will now be the
events leading up to the establishment of the first Olympic
Games. The transition to this theme is effected with the greatest subtlety. The Cycnos-Heracles battle had been rejected
as a melody by the imposition of the victory of Hagesidamos,
which blots out the expected second encounter while at the
same time, although in a present multiform, it states that
event. But the act is now an Olympic victory. In summary
fashion the causes are reviewed: the trainer's activity and
the protégé's own dedication to his task. The poet will therefore sing the appropriate honor, an Olympic ode. This particular type of ode will itself become a theme at the completion
of the mythic section, when, as we have seen, the inau-

243

gural ceremonies culminate in the birth of eulogy. Within
this outer framework, the subject is again Heracles, but the
transition passage has worked to redirect our focus to the
Olympic activity of that hero; that is to say, the curtailed
minor statement has reemerged in a strong major tonality.

The organization of the mythic material contains a poetic
ruse which fulfills, in a surprising form, the poet's earlier
promise of payment with interest, the secondary elaboration
of his opening pretense to have forgotten his debt:

> The future has caught up with me,
> Has called my deep debt due.
> Yet the dunning bite is dulled when interest too
> Is paid. The pebble is spun, washed
> By the churning wave: just so
> My poem will liquidate
> Indebtedness to friendship.

We shall see that the mythic material will present us with
this interest accrued to the poet's debt. The structural organization is that of the typical retrograde chronology. From the
event of Heracles' dedication of the altars by Pelops' tomb,
we regress to the death of Cteatos and Eurytos, the sons of
Poseidon and Molione and the nephews of Augeas, whose
stables Heracles had cleaned as one of the labors he had performed in the service of Eurysthenos. Augeas had refused
Heracles payment (we might note that *he*, unlike the poet,
did not pay *his* debts) and the deaths of the uncle and
nephews were the unwilling wage exacted—we might almost say, the wage with interest. But this was the second encounter of Heracles with the Molionidae. In the first, a further
step in retrograde chronology, they had defeated the army
of Heracles. The movement now reverses and retraces the
same events with greater elaboration. The death of Augeas,
narrated in striking colors, is followed by the full description
of Heracles' dedication of the altars at Olympia. The concen-
tric circles are complete; the expectation of structure has

been satisfied. It is true that Pindar has not yet treated the theme of the birth of eulogy, but it had been so obliquely touched upon in its first statement that it is not clear that this will be a theme until it emerges in its second elaboration.

The material that intervenes between the establishment of the altars and the birth of eulogy constitutes the accrued interest to the poet's debt. It is marked by the epic-parody questions which signal the forthcoming astounding memory-feat:

> Who was it won
> The initial wreaths:
> For boxing? for foot-race?
> For chariot? Who bet his honor on the Games
> And matched his signal boast with victory?

It is, however, only in a superficial sense that this section is extra-structural, for not only does it serve as transition to the birth of eulogy and therefore complete that structural unit, but it also realizes the significance of the poet's opening use of the rhetorical art of memory.

If, then, the catalog of victors is a material presentation of the interest accrued, it yet remains for another section of the poem to offer the expected second elaboration of the theme in an exquisite flight of fancy. In Greek, the word for interest is a metaphorical use of the word for "that which is born," or a child, a usage similar to Shakespeare's "*breed* of barren metal." The tardy poem is now the long-awaited son for which the aged father has almost given up hoping:

> A song from Dirce —late,
> But like the heir legitimate
> The father craves whose road is backward far from youth,
> And his heart is warmed with love; for if estates
> Devolve to shepherds, alien,
> Not of the blood,
> One's death is bitter.

The primary meaning of the word is now dominant; its metaphorical usage has, however, determined the terms of the extended simile, for it is not only the child but the child as
inheritor of wealth. The father could, of course, be Archestratos, but more probably it is Hagesidamos himself who
plays this poetic role. His own youthfulness need offer no ob-
struction to this imaginative variation. The poem has shown,
by his own position in the mental catalog, that Hagesidamos
is the legitimate heir to Olympia's glory. His death therefore
will not be bitter nor his splendor mortal. But it immediately
becomes evident that the victor's death is only the darker
foil for his final epiphany; the poet's love, like that of Zeus
for Ganymede, will redeem him, perhaps, from even that
common end. The impression of him at Olympia in his beauty
is now revealed as the iconograph "placed" in the poet's
memory.

In a larger sense, the child is not only the present poem
but its prototype, the original Olympic poem that was born
after the inaugural ceremonies. Pindar's insistence that the
present poem is sung at Zeus's behest will mean that his ode is
particularly Olympic in its subject matter. The myth relates
the foundation of the Olympic Games; and their patron deity,
Zeus, forms the subject of the epitome version of the present
ode which, as Pindar claims, follows the ancient precedent:

> .... sing
> The eponym of victory's Victory: Thunder and Bolt
> Of Fire in the Hand
> Of Zeus, who detonates
> The incandescent lightning
> That marks omnipotence.

At the close, Zeus reappears as the parent of the Muses, so
that the poet and the god stand in an especial relationship:

> But you
> Sweet lyre and flute asperge,

While tend your glory
Daughters Pierian
Of Zeus.

The poet's love and that of Zeus are thus easily confused and the paradigm of Ganymede imposes most delicate instruction on the heart of Zeus. It was, furthermore, the personification of Truth as daughter of Zeus that the poet had earlier invoked as guardian of his entire conceit.

With such far-flung fantasy, then, has Pindar embodied the simple cliché of the epinician ode: that the patron's victory entails the poet's debt.

Olympia X: For Hagesidamos of Western Locris: Victory in Boxing, Boys' Division

---

ΤΟΝ ΟΛΥΜΠΙΟΝΙΚΑΝ ΑΝΑΓΝΩΤΕ ΜΟΙ

THEME I

(strophe)

An Olympic victor —read off
My mind his name there written—
Ah, Archestratos' son: I owed him song, sweet song,
And had forgot. But, Muse, and you, Zeus'
Daughter, Truth, fend off
And thwart the lie
I failed a friend.

THEME II

(antistrophe)

The future has caught up with me,
Has called my deep debt due.
Yet the dunning bite is dulled when interest too
Is paid. The pebble is spun, washed
By the churning wave: just so

Olympia X

My poem will liquidate
Indebtedness to friendship.

(epode)

And why? Scrupulosity lives in Western Locris;
Calliope is all their care
And Ares, all abronze.

TRANSITION TO THE MYTH

To fight

With Cycnos was too much
For even Heracles: but then ... A boxing victory
At Olympia —thank Ilas,
Hagesidamos; so Patroclos
Did Achilles.
Hone a man to excellence: you rouse him
With god's help to fame gigantic.

(strophe)

But few or none uncommitted
Win life's light, this act
Of acts, this game surpassing,

THEME III

that I sing at Zeus' behest.

MYTH: TIME 3

By Pelops' antique tomb, six
Altars had been founded after

MYTH: TIME 2

Poseidon's perfect
Cteatos was slain

(antistrophe)

And slain was Eurytos, the wage
Exacted willy-nilly from the haughty
Augeas: from ambush near Cleonae it was they he
    waylaid —
Who? why, Heracles! And why? Once

249

MYTH: TIME 1

Before, these proud Molionidae
Had stormed the army
From Tiryns he had encamped

(epode)

At Elis.

MYTH: TIME 2

Ha! For perfidy, for fraud, for exploitation,
That Epeian king soon after
Saw his country's wealth,
His city sinking
Under solid flame and slash of iron deep
In the ditch of ruin.
La raison des plus forts
Est toujours la meilleure.
And he, in his stupidity, the last encountered
And caught, plunged down death's cliff.

(strophe)

MYTH: TIME 3

The puissant son of Zeus
Reviewed his regiments at Pisa
With all their booty; plotted out the father of fathers'
    holy
Place; and on the consecrated ground he palisaded
Altis; the environ's crops
He destined for the temple;
And elevated Alpheos-ford

(antistrophe)

To the rank of the Twelve Deities;
And named Cronos-Hill. (Before,
When Oenomaos ruled, it had no name, was blizzard
    and snow.)
These inaugural ceremonies the Destinies
Attended and he that is

Olympia X

Alone who tests
Veracity — I mean

(epode)

Time, whose forward path announces what is clear:
Heracles divided war's
Gift and sacrificed the best;
Established the quadrennial
Festivity with Olympia's first contest and its trophies.

TRANSITION TO THE CATALOG

Who was it won
The initial wreaths:
For boxing? for foot-race?
For chariot? Who bet his honor on the Games
And matched his signal boast with victory?

(strophe)

CATALOG OF VICTORS

The two-hundred-yard dash:
First prize to Licymnios' son,
OIONOS.

> (He had come with the troops he marched from
> Midea.) The wrestling

Bout:
ECHEMOS,

who glorified Tegea.

DORYCLOS,

of the city Tiryns,
Took the boxing
Championship. The quadriga:

(antistrophe)

From Mantinea,
SAMOS,

Halirothios'

Son. The javelin:
PHRASTOR,

251

With a bull's-eye. And discus:

NIKEUS

circled, hurled

the stone
The winning length;

THEME III

his comrades were fired
To applaud. Evening, then.
Ablaze. Moonlight.
The beauty. And calm.

(epode)

Song all the sanctum filled in festivals
Of revelry: the eulogy was born,
Which ancient precedent we follow
Now and sing
The eponym of victory's Victory: Thunder and Bolt
Of Fire in the Hand
Of Zeus, who detonates
The incandescent lightning
That marks omnipotence. Sensuous movements
Of the dance enhance the flute's continuo,

(strophe)

THEME II

A song from Dirce —late,
But like the heir legitimate
The father craves whose road is backward far from
    youth,
And his heart is warmed with love; for if estates
Devolve to shepherds, alien,
Not of the blood,
One's death is bitter;

(antistrophe)

And . . . should sterile splendor
Go to Hades' steading

Olympia X

Unsung, a man, Hagesidamos, has drawn breath only to
  strive
At emptiness for transitory joy.

THEME I

                                        But you

Sweet lyre and flute asperge,
While tend your glory
Daughters Pierian

                                        (epode)

Of Zeus. Their zeal I second; his Locrian race
Embrace; in honey steep
This noble town. And praise
The son Archestratos
Loves: I saw him box and win there
By Olympia's altar,
That time ago,
In body's age
And beauty tempered just like Ganymede,
Whom Love redeemed from heartless death.

Isthmia V: Sunlight at Salamis

The historian who, in his search for documents about the great battle at Salamis, in which the Greeks defeated the naval force of the Persian Xerxes, reads the Fifth Isthmian ode, written by Pindar for Phylacidas of Aegina, is invariably disappointed to find so little information presented; it is unfortunate that the historian has conveyed his disappointment to the literary critic, who attempts to find some biographical reason for Pindar's apparent lack of enthusiasm for an event so significant for Greece. Biographical inventions have abounded, but they all incorporate two basic flaws: they assume, first, that a contemporary desires as detailed an account as today's ancient historian; and they accept the incongruity of a poet's signaling in a commissioned work his own tepid zeal for his patron's cherished subject, although such a duplicity would be tantamount to Bach's composing the *B Minor Mass* to confess in secret his own supposed atheism. The passage in question occurs in the last third of the ode:

> . . . . Ajax' city might testify
> Its sailors set it aright in War —
> Salamis, I mean, when Zeus rained carnage,
> The hail of death for countless men.

There is indeed little there for the historian, but we shall see that this passage is the very nucleus of the poem, and that without the radiant vision of what had happened at Salamis, the ode would lack what moderate beauty it has. Salamis determines the structure of the ode, but Salamis is not Phylacidas; there is therefore a deflection away from the proper recipient of encomium; and this deflection, we may postulate, was occasioned by the fact that Salamis, and not Phylacidas, struck in the poet's mind metaphysical reverberations. We might even say that Salamis meant too much to the poet, not too little, and consequently marred the poem's effectiveness as a particular encomium. The best poems of Pindar occurred when the athletic event gathered all the rays into itself.

The mention of Salamis is immediately followed by a variation of the break-off formula:

> Enough! Deluge with silence extravagant
> Speech: Zeus gives;
> Zeus takes away, Zeus, King of all.

We can understand the statement only with reference to the lengthy introduction to the Salamis nucleus. Pindar had claimed that great warriors have been the theme for poets, and in illustration he had cited a catalog of various heroes and the peoples who sang their fame. The catalog had ended with Aegina and the sons of Aeacos, who had taken Troy in two separate campaigns. Troy induces for Pindar an extreme excitement, and he feigns a desire to tell the whole story. The questions which follow are actually the beginning of that narrative, for they are in parody of the epic style:

> Take wing; the beginning sing:
> Who was it killed Cycnos, who
> Hector, and the Aethiop general,
> Intrepid Memnon, bronzed for war? And who
> Impaled good Telephos at the banks of the Caïcos?

The reply he offers to the series of questions is Aegina, the country which here stands collectively for the warriors who came from there. Although the answer to the questions should have set the subject for narrative, the collective answer means that the poet must still select what aspect he will treat in a leisurely fashion. He could, as he says, choose some item in Aegina's epic past, some theme that has already been treated by previous poets:

> .... a tower of lofty
> Paramountcy built is ours to climb:
> The well-known arrows
> Are many my tongue could cascade in their praise.

He bypasses the items of myth, however, and chooses an event from contemporary history. The event is, of course, the battle of Salamis. In such a context, it is announced as the present subject that is to receive epic elaboration. Salamis is today's Trojan war. He could have granted the battle no higher honor than this juxtaposition in which Salamis is superimposed upon the past epic material. It is not the amount of time the poet spends in narrating the events of Salamis that is important, but rather the careful contextual preparation for the announcement of the theme. In fact, the shortness of the mention is part of the honor; for the glory of its position is intensified by the *recusatio* in which the poet dares not, for fear of upsetting the balance which has been established in the vicissitudinal nature of the universe, actually embark on his proposed epic. An epic, moreover, would be a dissonant digression for the epinician genre; and Pindar had prefaced the entire crescendo to the Salamis nucleus by saying that no praise for Aegina would be too great, provided it be suitable for the format of the ode:

> But have it taken
> The thoroughfare of high deeds god has given,
> Begrudge it then no flourished toast
> Too lofty for this ode.

He had begun soberly enough by justifying, by the catalog, his inclusion of warriors as subject matter for eulogy, but—so, at least, is the implied conceit—he had forgotten himself in his extravagant enthusiasm. The epinician ode, therefore, when he returns to it after the curtailed narrative, becomes a pis aller; the sailors of Salamis will enjoy the ode, since they cannot have the epic:

> Such excellence enjoys no less
> Balm epinician, this ode.

The confusion of athlete with warrior is, of course, a common metaphor for Pindar; it was this cliché that perhaps suggested his structural conceit. The point here, however, is not that the athlete is being compared to a warrior, but that the warrior is receiving the athlete's poem.

The athletes in this poem are only a springboard to the Salamis narrative, and when they return at the end of the curtailment, they merely satisfy the ring-structure frame for the nucleus; their perfunctory praise pales before the glory which has preceded; their encomium is almost taken from them and presented to the sailors of Salamis as a consolation prize for their unwritten epic.

The final awarding of the crown at the end of the ode returns to the opening invocation in which the athlete's wreath had been described. Here too, however, it is Salamis that is uppermost in the poet's mind, for the vision of sunlight on water inspired, no doubt, the magnificent hymn to the mother of the Sun. It is she who glances off gold and gives it its supremacy among the other elements. In a parallel enumeration, it is also she who is reflected from warring ships on the sea or chariots that battle on land. Third in the series is the glory of the athlete, whose achievement also is bathed in such divine light. But what should be the culminating position becomes, in the context of the whole ode, something less than that; for even the commonplace about success with which the opening hymn ends will come to have more meaning for the warriors of Salamis and their narrative, which had come too close to an overreaching aspiration:

> Only
> These two cultivate life's choicest
> Flower in the garden of prosperity's abundance:
> Success and hearing praise of one's success.
> Never seek to be a Zeus: already all
> Is yours if those two blessings come your way;
> For man to man's estate must acquiesce.

Isthmia V: For Phylacidas of Aegina, Pancratiast

ΜΑΤΕΡ ΑΛΙΟΤ ΠΟΛΤΩΝΤΜΕ ΘΕΙΑ

STROPHE

Who bore the sun, Divineness, we call you many
Names, and who why universal gold
Of elements is standard held in primacy:
Look! Warring
Ships on sea and harnessed horse of war —
You, Our Queen, we see there dazzle,
You, as contest tides and turns.

ANTISTROPHE

And games of athletes, too: he wins the yearned-for
Fame whose hair in tiers of crowns
Is bound; for hands have triumphed or feet
Have raced the swiftest:
Something of divinity is judge when we excel. Only
These two cultivate life's choicest
Flower in the garden of prosperity's abundance:

EPODE

Success and hearing praise of one's success.
Never seek to be a Zeus: already all

Is yours if those two blessings come your way;
For man to man's estate must acquiesce.

Isthmus, Phylacidas, records your flowerage
In pancration; Nemea doubles the championship,
Both yours and Pytheas'. My heart,
If not for Aeacids, has no taste for song;
With Eloquence for Lampon's sons I come

STROPHE

Here to a city that law has ordered.
                                        But have it taken
The thoroughfare of high deeds god has given,
Begrudge it then no flourished toast
Too lofty for this ode;
In past magnificence, great warriors too song made
The greater, famed through lyres while all
The voices of the flutes consort in jubilee

ANTISTROPHE

Time without end: they venerated set —so Zeus
Ordains— a theme for poets. To wit:
Aetolians honor by flames of sacrifice
The puissant sons
Of Oeneus; Thebes, the chariot driver Iolaos;
Argos, Perseus; who live on the banks
Of Eurotas, Castor's spearmanship and Polydeuces';

EPODE

But here Wine Island's subject is the proud,
The spirited temperament of Aeacos and his sons: they too
    were warriors,
Twice sacked the city of Troy, first
In the company that followed Heracles, then
With the Atreidae. Take wing; the beginning sing:
Who was it killed Cycnos, who
Hector, and the Aethiop general,

Isthmia V

Intrepid Memnon, bronzed for war? And who
Impaled good Telephos at the banks of the Caïcos?

STROPHE

And answers my mouth, "Aegina, their country, this island
Far-seen on the sea": a tower of lofty
Paramountcy built is ours to climb:
The well-known arrows
Are many my tongue could cascade in their praise; today
A new one: Ajax' city might testify
Its sailors set it aright in War —

ANTISTROPHE

Salamis, I mean, when Zeus rained carnage,
The hail of death for countless men.

Enough! Deluge with silence extravagant
Speech: Zeus gives;
Zeus takes away, Zeus, King of all.
Such excellence enjoys no less
Balm epinician, this ode.

> Athletes,

EPODE

Contend who dare with the clan Cleonicos
Sired: the magnitude of their exertion only blind men
Could not see, nor what expense provoked
The fair expectation of their hopes. As gymnast,
Too, Pytheas I praise: he steered
The course and style of Phylacidas' fists;
His hands are dexterous as his mind.

Take up his crown; bring him the woolen chaplet;
Release my fledgling hymn to flight!

Isthmia VI: "Beauty—Dangerous"

With remarkable insight, Gertrude Stein observed that a work of creative genius is characterized by a certain admixture of what we would ordinarily call the ugly. The application to her own work is, of course, obvious, although she good-heartedly included others, like Picasso, in her group. It is probably this prideful attitude that has turned so many away from her writings, for it is so easy to become bored with her repetitions, or to think that any child could do as well. And yet we may ask ourselves if, for example, there is anything in English that so closely approximates the finished calm of Homer as the early narrative style of Gertrude Stein, where, for a different reason, parataxis and incantatory ennui elevate the narrative segment to the function of a poetic element. Frequent recurrence of an inane prepositional phrase —or even a subtle observation— does not indicate her poverty of expression but acts as a clausula, dividing the prose into sections larger than the word; and these begin to delight us with the full force of rhythm and recognition.

Ugliness in what should be beautiful betrays the artist's struggle with recalcitrant material. The material, however, is recalcitrant for him alone, for it was his choice to make the form do what it had not done before. It would have been easier for Pindar and for us, had he been Bacchylides rather than himself. New genius is a taste that is acquired; we have been some generations in calming our nerves to the jangling of Schönberg. But the step forward is irreversible, and once the artist has conveyed his vision, we must eventually look back in boredom at what he could so easily have done but did not. We come to realize that it is in the very ugliness that resides the beautiful.

The artist himself is not always avant-garde, but, for whatever reasons, sometimes more fully satisfies his contemporaries' expectations. These are the works that please but do not transport, the works preferred by those who do not like the author but think they do (Schönberg's *Verklärte Nacht* will serve as our illustration). It is thus that we come, in conclusion, to another poem Pindar wrote for an Isthmian victory of the Aeginetan, Phylacidas.

"Isthmia VI" presents no asperities; once one has come to recognize the various elements that combine to orchestrate the patron's eulogy in an epinician ode, one reads this poem with thorough understanding. The magnificent opening not only incorporates a particular conceit but also determines the mythic section and reappears in the close. The banquet scene, as in the poem for Diagoras of Rhodes, suggests the metaphor. At the high point of the celebration, the poet offers his toast to the victor: "A second round of toasts," for a son of Lampon has already won before; and Pindar, at the time, had apparently written that ode too —the poem numbered "Nemea V" in the Pindaric corpus. The banquet traditionally includes three toasts, the third round addressed to Olympian Zeus the Savior. The poet's second round, therefore, implies, as he will himself make explicit, the third; and Phylacidas, who has won at a minor game, will, if the sequence of toasts is to be believed, yet in the future win at the great Olympian contest. The narrative section also presents a toast, also one that looks to the future. The theme is an event in the first taking of Troy; in the expected manner, a summary account gives place to a brighter focus on one moment in the myth. Heracles comes to Aegina to impress Telamon into the expedition; he finds the company at banquet and is asked to join the festivities. His acceptance becomes the toast he offers to Olympian Zeus, in which he asks that the god allow Telamon's wife, Eriboea, to conceive a son. The son will be Ajax, who will sail to Troy in the second expedition; and the child's name is suggested by the omen that Zeus sends to signal his acceptance of the toast, "the bird/ Imperial, King eagle," whose name in Greek provokes the pun on "Aiglon Ajax." The poem modulates back to the opening banquet-scene and the ode itself becomes the toast; wine is transmuted to the sacred water of the Theban spring, Dirce, a sphragistic indication for Pindar's poetry. The thirst for praise, first suggested in actuality by the training athlete's thirst for water, becomes his motivating aspiration, and is satisfied no longer by wine or water but by the ode that celebrates his glory. And as the recipient of praise is broadened to a national significance, his thirst is rewarded by the asperges cast on Aegina itself; his garden that divinity has planted in fame and joy becomes the thirsting land that awaits the rain from heaven:

> How excellent this dew of elegance, this water
> Fallen on Psalychid land!

A neat progression, like a series of chordal harmonies, introduces the Heracles myth. There are so many splendors in the history of Aegina, "such facets for cantata," as he will later say, the poet has before him an *embarras du choix*:

> For myriad roads fan out
> And each a highway high deeds cut,
> Beyond the sources of the Nile,
> Beyond who live with the Northern Wind.
> No one is so foreign, nor city's speech so backward,
> It have not heard how into divinity
> Peleus magnificent married.

No, everyone has heard of Peleus; everyone has heard of Ajax; everyone has heard of Telamon; and the theme is thus placed in focus. The leisurely narrative, once well under way, is curtailed by a variation of the device which we have no trouble in recognizing as the break-off formula; the chordal progression returns us to the subjects of the present eulogy:

> But hold! I have not time
> To tell of so much excellence. Phylacidas,
> Pytheas, Euthymenes —intendant of their revels,
> Muse, I come. And be it said laconically!

The victory-catalog is of modest length, since apparently their victories have not been spectacular, even if one includes the uncle, Euthymenes. There is here, however, no opportunity, as in "Isthmia V," to seek a cosmic significance; and the catalog yields precedence to a piece of Hesiodic exegesis, which serves as a pretext for extolling the athletes' father, Lampon, who, like a hone, has sharpened his sons to high achievement.

We see here what we have come to expect: introduction, transition, relevant myth, break-off formula, victory-catalog, particular eulogy, gnomic passages, textual exegesis, and widened festivity occasioned by the victory. The poem is coherent, although somewhat low-keyed; it is competent; it is perhaps even slick. It is, we might add, an early poem, probably predating "Isthmia V" with its mention of the battle of Salamis. But later poems sometimes show as well the same professional assurance. What we miss is the ugliness, the grotesque exaggeration of some element, the wild daring in elaboration and variation, the form that continues to ring on into metaphysical eddyings. If we have come to appreciate Pindar's genius, such a beautiful but not dangerous ode merely turns us back to read again the imperfections of his truer greatness.

Isthmia VI: For Phylacidas of Aegina, Pancratiast

ΘΑΛΛΟΝΤΟΣ ΑΝΔΡΩΝ ΩΣ ΟΤΕ ΣΥΜΠΟΣΙΟΥ

STROPHE

Banquet's vendage: a second round
Of toasts, this krater, wines of Music's lines
Composed —"To the athletes, Lampon's
Sons!" One, O Zeus, at Nemea —
Yours was the wreath that flowered his poem;
And now, you Isthmian Lord
And fifty Nereids: Phylacidas, the younger
Son, has won. Here's to the toast,
The third, "Our Savior, Olympian!" raised
To Aegina in choired mellisonance.

ANTISTROPHE

For look: a man spares no expense
And works to build his excellence on god's foundation;
His garden divinity plants
In fame and joy: in the orient of happiness,
Say, he has cast his anchor; is god's

Isthmia VI

Elect. Such to be
And greet his death or greying age
Here prays Cleonicos' son. O Spinstress
To Heaven's Throne, grant with your sister
Fates my friend's claim to splendor.

EPODE

O sons of Aeacos, O gold of chariot,
How clearer could my mandate be:
Draw near this island; asperge cast of eulogy.
For myriad roads fan out
And each a highway high deeds cut,
Beyond the sources of the Nile,
Beyond who live with the Northern Wind.
No one is so foreign, nor city's speech so backward,
It have not heard how into divinity
Peleus magnificent married;

STROPHE

Nor heard of Telamon's Ajax; ha!
Not heard of even Telamon: how to battles'
Bronze disports as Tiryns'
Forward ally in their fleet at Troy,
Where champions anguished —ah, Laomedon's
Perfidy!— Alcmene's son
Brought him; took Pergamon; joined him to kill
The Merops nation and the oxherd like a mountain,
Alcyoneus, he found in Phlegra; nor spared
Their hands the bows' twanged strings —

ANTISTROPHE

That Heracles! It had begun with Aeacos' Telamon
Impressed to sail: he had found him banqueting and stood
    there
In his lion skin; was asked
The first to pour nectareal libation,
Amphitryon's Heracles, I mean, the lancer;

267

Was handed the wine in goblet,
Gold in repoussé, by splendid Telamon.
He elevated it to heaven in the brawn of his hands;
He spoke: "If ever, O Father Zeus,
Your heart was pleased to hear my prayers,

EPODE

Hear me now: let Eriboea now,
I beg, conceive this man
A healthy son; my friend fulfil his destiny.
May its strength —like the hide
That mantles me, the prize I killed for first
Original contest at Nemea—
No way break; may courage not lag
Behind!" God sent his answer, the bird
Imperial, King eagle; the joy
Provoked moved Heracles

STROPHE

To speak like a man of prophecy: "You shall have
The son you long have prayed for, Telamon; and the bird
That has appeared, give him its name:
Reach of eagles, Aiglon Ajax,
Lord of hosts in the service of War."
Thus he spoke; then took
His seat. But hold! I have not time
To tell of so much excellence. Phylacidas,
Pytheas, Euthymenes —intendant of their revels,
Muse, I come. And be it said laconically!

ANTISTROPHE

Here then: they took three trophies for pancration
At Isthmus and others where forests shade Nemea —
These princely sons, their uncle.
Such facets for cantata they hold up to the light!
How excellent this dew of elegance, this water
Fallen on Psalychid land!

Isthmia VI

House of Themistios, hold up your head:
God loves the city where they dwell. Lampon
Perfects through practice; approves that verse
Of Hesiod; recites and recommends it to his sons.

EPODE

The glory he produces the town all shares;
And guests esteem his hospitality.
The middle course he plans, pursues; the middle course he
    holds.
His tongue does not outstrip his mind:
Call him a Naxian whetstone, the hone
For bronze; so fine he edges
Others to athletics. I drink their health then,
This sacred Dirce water, that pour by Cadmos'
Fortress gates gold-gowned Memory's
Daughters, their robes sashed high.